TRIED BY FIRE

TRIED
BY FIRE

Expositions
of the First
Epistle of Peter

F. B. Meyer

OLIPHANTS

OLIPHANTS
BLUNDELL HOUSE
GOODWOOD ROAD
LONDON S.E.14

First Lakeland Edition 1970

SBN 551 00077 5

PRINTED IN GREAT BRITAIN BY
WILLMER BROTHERS LTD, BIRKENHEAD
AND BOUND BY C. TINLING & CO. LTD, PRESCOT

Contents

PREFACE

These Expositions do not attempt to be critical or exhaustive; but the aim has been to deduce such spiritual exhortations and consolations from the glowing words of the Apostle as will most readily help Christian people in the varied circumstances of daily life.

Delivered first as Expositions in the course of my stated ministry, they were afterwards published week by week in the pages of *The Christian*; and in response to very many requests are here preserved in a permanent form.

It has never been my plan in regular exposition to burden the minds of my hearers with all the different opinions of commentators on the varied points arising for discussion in almost every paragraph. It has been my habit rather to read everything within my reach, and then to state my own general conclusions as simply and clearly as possible. This method has been followed in the present case.

Leighton's admirable Commentary on 1 Peter (now out of print) has been of considerable use, and I have enriched my chapters with several extracts from this mine of spiritual wealth. Indeed, wherever quotation marks occur without reference to the name of the author, the reader may conclude that they indicate passages culled from this source. I trust that I have acknowledged all my indebtednesses where the *ipsissima verba* have been used: but who of us can trace the source of ten thousand thoughts which by use we have come to appropriate as our own!

Written amid the multiplied engagements of a busy life, it would be impossible to estimate the benefit to heart and thought by bending over these translucent depths of sacred truth—so calm, so still, so profound, so counteractive of life's feverish haste; and it is my earnest hope that these Expositions may pass on to others some of the blessedness which their preparation has brought myself.

F. B. MEYER

1

THE PRELUDE

"Peter, an apostle of Jesus Christ, to the strangers scattered throughout Pontus, Galatia, Cappadocia, Asia, and Bithynia; elect according to the foreknowledge of God the Father, through sanctification of the Spirit unto obedience and sprinkiling of the blood of Jesus Christ: Grace unto you, and peace, be multiplied."—1 PETER 1:1, 2.

This Epistle was the child of many tears and of much sorrow. It was written probably about the year A.D. 65, when the followers of Jesus of Nazareth were regarded with growing dislike, whilst clouds of suffering and persecution were passing over the house of God (4:17). The disciples had already begun to learn by bitter experience that they were to follow their Master's steps by way of the *Via Dolorosa* to the light of the Resurrection morn; and that they must not expect softer names or usage than had been accorded to Him. They needed comfort; a stimulus to patience; a recital of the arguments for heroic endurance—all of which the Spirit of God supplied through these fervid and persuasive paragraphs.

And thus there is hardly any portion in the Word of God which has been more eagerly read than this Epistle, by those who were pressed with many trials and weaknesses. By exiles in the distant lands, shut out from all human tendernesses; by travellers and voyagers; by persecuted and suffering saints, hunted into the dens and caves of the earth, or immured in the living rock and beneath the boom of the ocean wave; by those whom sore sickness or venerable age may have incapacitated from meeting with the visible church—these words have been lovingly pondered and treasured, as a priceless heritage.

To a student of the earlier life of the Apostle Peter it would have seemed in the highest degree unlikely that one so impulsive, so rough-handed, so fond of action, should have been selected to write some of the tenderest and most consolatory words that have ever fallen on the ears of suffering and persecuted saints. Yet so it befell. And we are left to infer how keenly this strong nature must have suffered before it could have become so sweetened and softened, so humble and tender, as to afford a tropic soil for the luxuriant growth of the balsam and spicery of Divine comfort. Very different was this Apostle of Jesus Christ, when he wrote this Epistle, from the fisherman who girded himself in early life to his toils —from the disciple who abandoned all to follow the Master with enthusiastic ardour. Age had diminished the writer's strength, taken the sparkle from his eye, sown his head with grey, and bowed his frame. His self-reliance had learnt to cling to a stronger than himself; his wisdom to defer to a wiser. The asperities and ruggedness of his character had been toned and mellowed by suffering and sorrow, as the tints of a picture are softened by the breath of the years. In the deepest sense he was "converted" at last, that he might set himself to strengthen his brethren (Luke 22:32).

We cannot now recover his hidden history, lost in the gulf which separates this Epistle from the moment when last we caught sight of him emerging from the prison at Jerusalem (Acts 12:9—11), or exciting the indignation of St. Paul at Antioch (Gal. 2:11). We have no certain record of how those years were spent. Though, since he speaks so familiarly to these saints scattered throughout Asia Minor, many of whom may have received their first impressions from his lips on the day of Pentecost (comp. first verse with Acts 2:9), we should judge that he travelled with his wife (1 Cor. 9:5) for some time throughout those regions, settling for a longer time in the new city, which was rising on the ancient site of Babylon (5:13). This Epistle was written there; and the countries mentioned are enumerated in the order which would naturally have suggested itself to one looking out on them from a commanding central position.

I. THE INSCRIPTION.—"To the Strangers of the Dispersion." These words clearly designate Jews as principally addressed. While as yet the site which was to be occupied by Rome was covered by but a few straggling huts within a rude enclosure, the King of Assyria was already engaged in carrying into exile the ten tribes of Israel (2 Kings 17:6 ff.). They were captives quite a cen-

8

tury and a half before Judah and Benjamin were transplanted to Babylon; and it does not appear that they, to any great extent, participated in the restoration decreed by Cyrus. They remained in the land of their adoption, whence many travelled in various directions until, at the time of the writing of the New Testament, they were found in all the principal cities of the world. These were the "Strangers of the Dispersion." Their speech, their garb, their physiognomy, their religious rites—marked them out as perfectly different from those around them, and identified them with the holy city and with that peculiar people whose name they bore.

Many of them had become Christians, not only through the influences experienced when visiting their national metropolis, the very atmosphere of which must have been impregnated with Christian thought; but also through the labours of the Apostle Paul, whose first efforts were always directed to his own people, and whose name must be for ever associated with the infant churches which he founded in the regions where so many of the Jews of the dispersion had settled.

But we must not limit the scope of these words to Christian *Jews*. There are phrases which demand a wider interpretation. That, for instance, which alludes to "former lusts" of those addressed (1:14); and that also which speaks of them as not having been "a people" in time past (2:10). Besides which, the term *strangers* is distinctly employed in a spiritual sense (2:11), and so applies equally to all who go out to Christ without the camp, bearing his reproach, and who confess that they have here no continuing city, but seek one to come.

Do we cultivate enough the spirit of the *stranger*? We know what it is to turn from the attractions of a foreign city, with its wealth of art, its churches and its picture galleries, its antique buildings, and the glitter of its modern boulevards, towards a tiny box of brick in a grimy street, which is endeared to us as *home*. We may not linger longer; we are going home. Or if we stay on from day to day, we hardly unpack our suitcases, and certainly do not secure a settled abode, because it is not our home. Nor are we too much troubled by the discomforts and annoyances of our hotel, or by the risings of popular excitement around. Of what consequence are such things to those who may indeed bestow a passing interest on events happening around them, but whose interests are elsewhere, in the place which, however humble, differs from all the world beside in being *home*?

Oh for more of the TENT LIFE amongst God's people! But it is only possible, when they catch sight, and keep sight, of "the city which hath foundations". When that city is a city of tradition or dream, men will begin to dig the foundations of permanent homes and ample fortunes. But when it is realised as the object of passionate persuasion, descried by faith rising above the mists and plains of time, and embraced by outstretched eager arms, they dwell in tents, and confess themselves strangers and pilgrims.

It is said that when, in a strange land, the Swiss soldier hears the rude melody which gathers the cows back from the pastures, he is so filled with longings for home that he will cast down his sword, tear off his foreign livery, renounce his claims for wage, in order to hurry back to his mountain home. Would that such an effect might be experienced, after a spiritual sort, by many readers of these lines; who, as we speak of the inheritance, shall also array their spirits in the pilgrim garb, and start, not as they did in the Middle Ages for the holy sepulchre, or in quest of the holy grail, but for the New Jerusalem, on which the hand of invasion has never fallen, nor sin left its blight!

II. THE SPIRITUAL DESIGNATION.—"Scattered in the countries, and yet gathered in God's election, chosen or picked out; strangers to men amongst whom they dwelt, but *known* and *foreknown* to God; removed from their own country, to which men have naturally an unalterable affection, but made heirs of a better."

Elect.—Before all worlds God chose us in Christ (Eph. 1:4). There is no election outside of Christ. He was chosen, and all who were one with Him, in a union which was before time, but which is manifested in the process of time. We know little or nothing of the secret transactions of Eternity; but we can tell if we were included in them by a very simple test. All whom the Father gave to Christ come unto Him (John 6:37). If, therefore, we have come to Christ, attracted to Him, as steel filings to the magnet, we may assure our hearts, and dare to lay claim to the blessings and responsibilities included within that mystic circle.

But notice to what we are elect!—We are elect to OBEDIENCE. Not merely that we should escape the penalty

10

due to sin, or that we should pass into a region where storms do not rave and sin does not molest. No, this is but a small thing in the history of our souls. We are elect to obey; elect to suffer, that through suffering we may become strong; elect to be the saviours, and helpers and priests, of other men, through a very baptism of blood and tears; elect to be nearest Christ, because resembling Him closely in ministry, and devotion, and love.

Election is no selfish thing.—Those who think it is, and who lay flattering unction to their hearts that they at least are right, and may therefore leave the world to its fate, are probably utterly deceived; or have only beheld the faintest glimmer of what God means by his high calling and choice. We are chosen to obey; to serve; to learn; to suffer; to die daily—that others may be blessed and saved. Elect stars shine—to illumine the night. Elect nations—to lead the van of the world's progress. Elect spirits, like Isaiah, Jeremiah, Paul, Luther, and Knox—to be the channels down which, at much cost to them, the grace of God may better reach the world beneath their feet.

According to the foreknowledge of God the Father.—From all eternity He knew those who would accept the overtures of mercy. Shall we say that He foresaw the certain affinity between the elect One and those who would cleave to Him by faith? And concerning all these, whom He foreknew, He also predestinated, determined, resolved, that they should be conformed to the image of his Son. To those who are really saved by faith in the Lord Jesus, there is an infinite source of comfort here, in knowing that—beneath all the changes of our moral and spiritual condition—outlasting time, strong as Omnipotence, tender and true as the heart of God, there is a Divine purpose which is pledged to carry us onwards to beauty of moral character, and an obedience which is fashioned after the pattern of Christ's (Rom. 8:29).

Through sanctification of the Spirit.—The election of the Father in eternity is made effectual through the work of the Holy Spirit in time. That which is election in the Father, appears as sanctification in the work of the Spirit. Sanctification is setting apart. The root idea of the word is just separation from common uses to the service of God. The saint is one who has separated himself from known evil in an act of consecration, which is prolonged through all his after-life; and who is animated

11

by but one aim and purpose—to be only for Jesus. We cannot do more than this; nay, we cannot do this without the Holy Spirit. From Him comes the first conviction that we are wrong; and the indication of the infirmity, or weight, or evil, from which we must get free. From Him also comes the grace by which we are set free. From Him comes the in-filling with the love and life of God, which is inseparably connected with each act of consecration. And thus there is evolved at last the obedience which pleases God; and which is thus wrought through —and in—sanctification of the Spirit.

Yield to the Spirit. Recognise his indwelling. Do what He commands, and forbear from doing aught that his still small voice forbids. Every such act of consecration to his will must lead to the fuller light, and love, and power which make up holiness. And out of all this there will unfold the fair life of obedience, which is the perfected blossom of the hidden subsoil root of election. Election, the root; the grace of the Spirit, the atmosphere; obedience, the flower.

Unto sprinkling of the blood of Jesus Christ.—Here, then, is the Trinity—Father Son, and Spirit—all engaged in the work of lifting us from the bondage of corruption into a life wherein we shall as much love to do right as now to do wrong.

Very fitly does this mention of the blood follow that of obedience, as if to remind us that the best obedience could not avail to save us apart from the precious blood, and that our best acts need sprinkling. "The very tears of the purest repentance, unless they be sprinkled with this blood, are impure. All our washings without this are but labour in vain" (Jer. 2:22; Job 9:30, 31).

How necessary that the prayer of the contrite Psalmist should not be far from our lips on our holiest days and after our best services! "Purge me with hyssop, and I shall be clean; wash me, and I shall be whiter than snow" (Psa. 51.).

III. THE SALUTATION, "Grace and peace be multiplied". —The Apostle here blends the Western and Eastern modes of salutation. The Greek used *grace,* the Hebrew *peace;* and whatever each meant was intended to be conveyed in this salutation.

Grace is the unmerited love of God, stooping to save and bless; the source of all those bright and holy gifts which come from his infinite heart. As one beam of light

12

will break into many colours, so does the grace of God disperse into the several priceless gifts of his grace; "grace upon grace," like ripples breaking in music on a silver strand.

Peace follows upon grace. There is first peace *with* God, and then the peace *of* God. We lay down our arms of rebellion, and are welcomed into the family, so that there is no longer discord or dispute. And then the very peace which dwelt in the heart of Jesus comes as a sentinel to our inmost being; and it garrisons our heart and mind.

Such is the heritage of the servants of the Lord. And there is no higher wish to be entertained for them, than that this grace and peace should be in them, and increase in geometrical progression, and so *be multiplied*.

2

THE INHERITANCE

"Blessed by the God and Father of our Lord Jesus Christ, which according to his abundant mercy hath begotten us again unto a lively hope by the resurrection of Jesus Christ from the dead, to an inheritance incorruptible, and undefiled, and that fadeth not away, reserved in heaven for you."—1 PETER 1:3, 4.

How little does the wailing infant, over whose cradle glistens the coronet first won by the stout arm of a soldier-ancestor, understand of the inheritance to which he has been born! The ancestral home, the far-spread lands, the noble rank, the prestige of an ancient and lofty lineage—all these things are his; but years must pass ere they can be truly realised or appreciated. And how much less do the most saintly and heaven-taught spirits conceive of that inheritance which is ours so soon as we become the children of God through faith in Jesus Christ![1] See how this fervent Apostle, though he would fain find words to tell us in what its bliss consists, is obliged to content himself with negatives. It is so much easier to say what the inheritance is not, than to set down the

13

elements of its exceeding weight of glory. It were easier far to enumerate all the ills of this mortal life, and to say of each, *This is not there,* than to give an inventory of all that awaits the saints, as one by one they pass through the veil, and find themselves in the land of their choice.

But surely, in dealing with the ungodly, it were well not only to dwell on the woes they must incur, but to insist on the glories they must miss unless they change their minds and repent. Ah! if only we could speak in terms glowing enough, tinged with the certainty and rapture of our own glad hopes concerning the fair land to which we are going, we should induce many a dweller in the City of Destruction to start with us on pilgrimage. But how can we talk with vivid conviction of that which occupies so small a space in our own inner life?

THE NATURE OF OUR INHERITANCE.—Many and varied descriptions might be given of it: *Salvation,* in its fullness and perfectness, which is ours in germ, but waits for its hidden glories of colour and form to be revealed in the summer that is coming (5, 9 ; Mark 13 : 28). *The City of God,* the vision of which, as its walls and pinnacles rose above the mists of time, allured the patriarchs forward, and made them content to dwell in frail and shifting tents. *Heaven,* with its cloudless light and sweet societies. *Glory,* as we shall see it on the face of our Emmanuel, and as it shall flood our own happy spirits.

But there is a deeper and more comprehensive view than any of these: one which includes them all ; as the ocean includes the seas, and bays, and straits, which, though known by separate names, are parts of its majestic and all-embracing fullness. In the law of the Jewish priesthood, "the Lord spake unto Aaron, Thou shalt have no inheritance in their land, neither shalt thou have any part among them. I am Thy part, and Thine inheritance, among the children of Israel" (Num. 18 : 20). It was a very satisfactory arrangement for the pious priest. He could well dispense with the oliveyards and vineyards, the cornfields and homesteads of Palestine, if he might have God to be the strength of his heart, and his portion for ever. And the Psalmist eagerly caught at the thought, gladly surrendering all portion in his life, if only he might be "satisfied" with God (Psa. 17 : 15). "The Lord is the portion of mine inheritance and of my cup: Thou maintainest my lot. The lines are fallen unto me in pleasant places; yea, I have a goodly heritage" (Psa. 16:5, 6).

Our inheritance is God Himself.—Not the golden harps. Not the sea of glass mingled with fire. Not rest from pain and immunity from sorrow. Not the blessed society of heaven. From all these, apart from God, we should at last turn away dissatisfied. They are but the accessories and embodiments of something deeper, more inward and rapturous—the possession of God. Heirs *of God, i.e.,* of all the communicable glories of the Divine nature. The Psalmist expressed the literal truth when he said, "Whom have I in heaven but Thee?" (73). To know Him, to explore his being, to live on his fullness, to discover new tracts and continents in the *terra incognita* of Godhead, to see his glory, to be changed into his image—this is "the heritage of the servants of the Lord."

Our inheritance begins here.—As a matter of right all God's nature is ours directly we are born into his family; as a vast tract of country, filled with woods and rivers and ore, belongs to the heir at the moment of birth. But, as a matter of fact, we shall never occupy all, even when eternity is passing over us; the finite can never really fully grasp the infinite. Yet, from the first moment of conversion, we may begin to enter on our inheritance. We commence by studying the inspired chart, which maps out that inheritance, and tells us what God is, and what He is prepared to be to us. Next we proceed to appropriate and make use of his attributes and properties for daily need. Then we become possessed of the indwelling Spirit of God, who brings his very nature into ours. And so we come to possess God just in proportion as He possesses us. We inherit Him as our portion up to the measure in which He inherits us. "The Lord is my portion, saith my soul." "The Lord's portion is his people."

Up! friends; you are living on a vast estate. Around you on all hands are God's love, and grace, and power, and wisdom, awaiting your use. Set yourself to know, and then to appropriate and enjoy. "There is much land yet to be possessed." Do not be content to be circumscribed and limited, as were the Danes by our great Alfred. Be rather like the early squatters in the Western States, who rolled back their fences, taking in evermore of the rich virgin soil, so adding field to field.

But our inheritance can only be perfected hereafter.— It is "reserved in heaven." We tire and faint amid our most rapturous experiences. The body refuses to sustain the weight of glory. The machinery of mortality breaks down beneath the pressure of the loftiest spiritual emotion. "I fell at his feet as dead." "Thou canst not see my face; for no man can see my face and live." And it may be that just as there are qualities in the universe which we cannot perceive because we have only five senses, so there are properties in God which we know not of because our powers of perception are limited. It is therefore quite conceivable that when clothed upon with our house which is from heaven, which will have a great many more windows in it than the earthly house of this tabernacle which is built for stormy weather, there will be sides and aspects of the Divine nature that we know nothing about to-day, but which shall be communicable and communicated to us.[2] Ah, fair inheritance! If earth and heaven, which are but as his vesture, are so lovely, what will He be!

THE QUALITIES OF THIS INHERITANCE.—*Incorruptible, i.e.,* as to its substance. It is not liable to decay. Nature looks her best in the days of early autumn. The golden cornsheaves; the gorgeous tints of the fading leaves; the berries of the wild rose and the rowan; the undiminished foliage of the forest trees; the ruddy wealth of the orchard: but, amid all, our enjoyment is tinged with sadness, for we know that decay lies beneath, eagerly at work; and that ere long the woodland glade will be strewn with the dying leaves, falling in myriads before the gale, and rotting in drenched heaps. So, too, amid our happiest converse with beloved ones, a sad foreboding sometimes invades our hearts, suggesting that it will not last: the artless child must leave the mother's embrace; the brother will choose another *confidante* than the sister whom he dearly loved. But the knowledge of God, like our treasure in heaven, cannot corrupt, nor can it be stolen from us by any thieving hand. It cannot pass from us; nor we from it. It cannot share the fate of any earthly possession. Nay, when we are stripped of all things else, and sit like another Job amid the wreck of former wealth, then we begin as never before to take measure of our eternal treasure; and there arises before us such a conception of the magnificence of our inheritance in God that we cry, "Give what Thou wilt! without Thee I am poor; and with Thee rich; take what Thou wilt away!"

Undefiled, i.e., as to its purity.—"All possessions here are defiled and stained with many defects and failings."

16

No marble without its flaw. No flower without its freckle.
No fruit without its blight. No face without its blemish.
No joy without its taint. No day without its regret. No
heart, except one, without sin. The leprosy of human
sin has so spread itself throughout the whole creation
that, as in Israel of old, garments and houses are alike
infected (Lev. 13, 14). And even in the purest earthly
friendships, a love which in its inception is innocent and
natural too often becomes tainted with jealousy and
selfishness, if not with pollution.

But to know God is to come into contact with the
source of Purity itself. "He that is near Me is near to
the fire" is a saying which an ancient writer puts into
the mouth of Christ. A wisp of straw might sooner survive the flame than defilement outlive contact with God.
"Neither shall evil dwell with thee." So far from our heritage becoming defiled, we cannot enjoy it unless we
love Purity. The pure in heart alone see God: and the
more they see of Him, the more pure they become.

Unfading, i.e., as to its beauty.—Here grows the amaranth, the flower that fades not. One never tires of what
is really beautiful. There is always some fresh expression
on a beautiful face, some new witchery of colour on
a beautiful landscape. We can easily understand how a
great preacher of this century, after some masterly effort,
would quiet his mind by taking from his pocket a hand-
ful of precious stones which he always carried there;
handling them, rolling them to and fro, holding them up
to the light, and never tiring of their ever-changing beauty.

There is all this in fellowship with God. To know Him
is a fountain of ever fresh delight. He never palls on the
satiated appetite. We never feel that there is monotony,
sameness, weariness, in his love. "All the happiness of
this life," said William Law, "is but trying to quench
thirst out of golden *empty* cups." But who shall speak
thus of the river of God's pleasure, which, as it gratifies
the thirst, increases it; which is ever more and better
than we could conceive; and which allures us on to
deeper and yet deeper draughts, to desires which grow
in being satisfied?

OUR TITLE TO THIS INHERITANCE.—"Begotten again." It
is not ours by merit; or by conquest; or by natural birth.
We may be the children of parents who have passed into
the skies; and yet we may miss the inheritance of the
saints in light. "Except a man be born again, he cannot

17

see the kingdom of God"; so said One who could not err. "If children, then heirs," is the indispensable order.

Nor is it difficult to see why it must be so. The inheritance is spiritual; and it requires spiritual faculties to apprehend and enjoy it. But in such as have not been born again those spiritual faculties are wanting. A blind man may stand amid the fairest landscape unconcerned, because the one organ by which he could enjoy it is wanting. A lunatic may live in a house stored with treasure of art and literature unaffected, because his mind is blank to all its attractions. And the unregenerate man might stand in heaven itself, and miss God, for want of those powers of spiritual perception of which he is deficient. Sin blinds the eye, stops the ear, and hardens the heart. The prime necessity is life; and life can only begin in the new birth.

We cannot possess God unless we love Him. We cannot love Him, unless there is a kinship and reciprocity of nature. But this nature is not ours by the first birth; and if it is to be ours at all, it can only be by the impartation of a new nature and life, which are the gift of God, through his Word (*ver.* 23).

Hast thou been born again? The certain sign is the faith which receives Christ. "As many as received Him, to them gave He the right to become children of God, even to them that believe on his name; which were born ... of God" (John 1:12, 13, R.V.).

THE LINK BETWEEN OUR PRESENT AND FUTURE.—"A living hope." We already have something of our inheritance, but at the best it is only the earnest—what the half-crown of the labourer in the feeing market is to the year's wage, or the sod of the estate to the broad acres. "Now through a glass darkly"—glimpses soon shadowed; outlines not filled up, dark sayings we cannot interpret.

But the time is coming when we shall know even as we are known, and see face to face; when our communion with God shall be as unfettered as our service; when we shall love Him better, and possess Him more fully. Towards this blessed consummation, as yet reserved, our hope stretches out both her hands; meanwhile, it is an inspiration and stimulus for every moment of our life. It is, indeed, "a living hope."

Hope is said sometimes to die: this never can. Sometimes though it lingers in the breast, it is inoperative: this is always quick and powerful. "Worldly hopes often mock men ; they are not living, but lying and dying ones. We live to bury them. But this hope answers our expectations to the full, and deceives in no way, but far exceeds them."

Its basis is "the resurrection of Jesus Christ from the dead."—The man who was once so hard to convince as he ran to the empty tomb, now realises the full meaning of that marvellous fact. Our Brother, Representative, and Lord, not only identified Himself with us in life and death, but has made us one with Himself in the Resurrection, which is also God's seal and Amen to all He said and did ; and is, therefore, a Divine corroboration not only of his words, but of all the structure of hope and expectancy which we have built on them.

THE ASCRIPTION OF PRAISE, with which this paragraph begins, is most befitting: "Blessed be the God and Father of our Lord Jesus Christ!"

Who shall compute the full measure of his abundant mercy? Mercy that He gave his Son to die and to rise again! Mercy that He has adopted us to a position which angels might envy ; because we are children, and therefore heirs! Mercy that He is willing to be the inheritance of such as we are! Mercy that He has given us such strong consolation, and an anchor so sure and steadfast! What multitudinous, infinite, inexpressible mercy! Let us bless Him for it, the Father of Jesus, and our Father in Him! Praise Him! praise Him!

"It is a cold, lifeless thing to speak of spiritual things on mere report ; but they that speak of them as their own, and as having some experience of their sweetness, cannot mention them, but their hearts are straight taken with such gladness as they are forced to vent in praises. This is such an inheritance that the very hopes and thoughts of it are able to sweeten the greatest griefs. What, then, shall the full fruition of it be!"

NOTES

[1] These opening sentences were suggested by one of Dr. Guthrie's sermons on *The Inheritance of the Saints*.

[2] Suggested by Dr. Maclaren.

3

"KEPT"

"Kept by the power of God through faith unto salvation."—1 PETER 1:5.

To have been told, as in the preceding verse, that our inheritance was "reserved in heaven" could have yielded us little comfort, unless that assurance had been followed and capped by this, that the heirs also are being kept for its full enjoyment. The sailor's most pressing question is not so much as to the welcome which awaits him in his home, but whether he can ride out the storm, and safely pass the jagged edges of the rocks, on which the waves are dashing angrily. You must assure him of safety for himself, as well as of welcome to his home, if you would put him perfectly at rest. So it were vain for the Apostle to talk of that "long eternity which shall greet our bliss with an individual kiss," unless he could also assure us that we shall be kept from making shipwreck, and becoming castaways. What comfort there is in that word "kept"!

The Greek word translated "kept" is borrowed from the camp. It is used in 2 Cor. 11:32; Gal. 3:23; Phil. 4:7; and, in each case, conveys the conception of an armed force, employed in sentry or escort duty, surrounding their ward, and interposing a wall of enclosure and defence. Thus does the Divine power surround the saints as a body-guard during their sojourn in this perilous world. God is not only our exceeding great reward, but our shield. The purged eye sees the mountains round about us filled with horses and chariots of protection. We are hidden in the secret of his presence from the pride of man, kept secretly in a pavilion from the strife of tongues. God hath sent out his light and truth to lead us, and bring us to his holy hill, and to his tabernacles. "Ye shall not go out with haste, nor go by flight: for the Lord will go before you; and the God of Israel will be your rearward."

20

It may be that many readers of these lines have come almost to despair. They know and approve the better, but do the worse. Notwithstanding bitter tears, and cries, and soul-anguish, they are constantly being brought into captivity to some besetting sin. How often have their tears been their meat day and night, as they have poured out their soul in the words of the fifty-first Psalm, or cried with the Apostle, "Oh, wretched man that I am, who shall deliver me?' For all such there is infinite comfort in the announcement that those who have been begotten again, and are therefore sons, may claim to be "kept" by their Father's power unto full and consummated salvation. Oh that from this moment all such may realise to the full the *keeping* power of God!

I. WHAT THIS KEEPING INVOLVES.—It does not mean that we shall lose our sinful nature ; which consists in a perpetual tendency and liability to sin. Nor does it mean that we shall become sinless beings, who need not the daily cry for forgiveness ; because in the best of us there must ever be much which is grievous in the sight of a holy God. Nor does it mean that we shall cease to be tempted ; *that* alas! cannot be our lot, as long as we are passing through an enemy's land to our inheritance. But it does mean that—though within us there is a strong predisposition toward sin, partly inherited and partly built up by long indulgence in evil habit, and though without us there is a hell full of wicked spirits, each of which is pledged to do his worst to make us fall—yet we may be kept from yielding to known and presumptuous sins, and conducted safely through the "proud waters," so as to stand at last with the OVERCOMERS on the shore of the sea of glass, having the harps of God. Not taken out of the world, but kept from the evil (Rev. 15 : 2 ; John 17 : 15).

Many are the images which suggest themselves to set forth the *keeping* power of God. What the framework of bone and the eyelid veil are to the delicate organism of the eye ; what the shepherd's watchful care is to the flock, which dwells safely in the wilderness, and sleeps in the woods, though young lions are roaring around for their prey ; what the lofty walls are to the tender grapes, guarding them from rifling hands and little foxes ; what the wing of the mother-bird is to the brood menaced by the hovering kestrel ; what the valiant of Israel were to Solomon's bed ; what the iron safe is to its valuable contents,

21

defying the robber's hand and the forked tongue of flame —all that is the environing presence of God to his saints. Though dogs compass us, and the assembly of the wicked inclose us, yet there is an inner circle of defence through which they dare not and cannot penetrate.

That there will be strife and war and temptation without, and cowering weakness within, seems implied in every one of these images, and especially in the metaphor we are considering. Of what need were KEEPING, unless there were danger without and frailty within? But amid all, it is evidently possible that we should be kept from stumbling; and spirit, soul, and body be preserved blameless unto the coming of our Lord Jesus Christ "Faithful is He that calleth you, who also will do it." This KEEPING extends to the issues of life, and to the steps or goings of the saints; but it touches these, because it deals so completely with the inner man. There the power of God is exerted on the soul, on the heart, and on the mind; unseen, but all-pervasive; and strong enough to quell the uprising of the wildest passion that ever swept down on the inner nature (Prov. 4:23; 1 Sam. 2:9; Phil. 4:7; 1 Pet. 4:19).

II. WHY THIS KEEPING MAY BE CONFIDENTLY EXPECTED. —*It is demanded by the purpose of God.*—We are "elect unto obedience," as the first verses of this chapter tell us; but surely He who has called us with so high a calling will not fail to deal effectually with all that would prevent it from being realised.

It is demanded by the sacrifice of Christ.—The expenditure of Calvary was gladly borne by our Saviour —not to deliver us from hell so much as "to purify unto Himself a people for his own possession, zealous of good works." But is it possible to suppose that the whole scheme of redemption is to be rendered abortive because, though He was able to purchase, He is not able to keep that which He has acquired? During his earthly life He kept those whom the Father had given Him, and none of them was lost, save the son of perdition, that the Scripture might be fulfilled; surely, then, since all power is now his, He is equally able to keep those who bear his name!

It is demanded by the indwelling of the Spirit.—He is most certainly in the heart of each believer; curtained, as of old was the Shekinah by the heavy veil, but still burning as a spark of fire in the most holy place. Above all things, He desires that the entire being, which is his temple, should be kept clean and holy. And if He only is permitted to have his way, He will most certainly reduce the inward chaos to order, and keep the inner empire undisturbed. Would it not be in the highest degree at variance with his loving holy nature to excite desires after holiness in the breast which He would not, or could not, meet? The very intensity of the passion for holiness which He instils is a pledge and harbinger of perfect satisfaction.

The credit of God demands it.—If sin must always master us, so long as we remain in this world, it would seem as if the remedy were not equal to the emergency. Here were indeed a subject for hellish merriment, if God were not able to counter-work the baleful influences which devils exert over human spirits. "Aha," methinks they would cry: "Thou canst make Thy saints obedient only by taking them beyond the range of our power; but leave them here within our reach, and Thou canst not keep them from yielding to the temptations which we present."

Take heart, O tempted child of God; thou hast abundant reason to reckon confidently on being "kept" from known transgression.

III. HOW THIS KEEPING IS EFFECTED.—"By the power of God."

Consider that power in creation.—Stand with the exiles in Babylon, and lift up your eyes on high to the starry hosts, spread out like a flock resting in the midnight sky: "He calleth them all by names, by the greatness of his might; for that He is strong in power: not one faileth." And if He can keep the heavenly bodies, revolving through orbits of measureless immensity, so exact to their hours that astronomers can calculate their return with unerring precision, surely He can keep one poor soul in its appointed orbit, especially when it is so eager to be kept (Isa. 40: 26).

Consider that power in history.—Notwithstanding the free action of human wills, warped and rebellious, He has been able to carry out his plans, and secure results on which He had set his mind from all eternity. And as a standing marvel the Israelite race remains to-day scattered among all peoples, but absorbed by none; isolated and alone, almost in spite of itself. But surely it must be as easy to preserve his Church, consisting as it does

23

of those who are exceedingly desirous of knowing and doing his will (Jer. 33: 25, 26).

Consider that power in the resurrection of our Lord. —It raised Him from the dead, past all created excellence, above principalities and powers, until the glorified but human body of Christ passed to the very throne of the Eternal, where no created thing had ever come before. Nay, but more—in raising Him, the Father also raised us in Him. And the Apostle tells us that the very same power which bore Christ from the grave to the throne is extended towards the weakest believer, to lift him also to a similar level of resurrection-being. Surely such a power as this is adequate to our direst necessity (Eph. 1: 19, 20).

Consider this power in the human life of Jesus.—He met the devil in the wilderness and in Gethsemane. The prince of this world measured himself in mortal conflict with the Son of God, not once only, but many times. But he was always defeated. His legions were driven forth from haunted lives. He himself fell as lightning from heaven. His head was bruised. His chief allurement and bait, the word, was overcome. His attempt to hold the Saviour in the tomb was defeated, as when a man brushes through the cobweb that stretches across his path. And what Jesus did for Himself, He waits to do on the behalf of each of his own, and to repeat in each of us the conquests and triumphs of his own life on earth.

It is hardly necessary to say that the power of God is put forth by the Holy Spirit.—He lives in our inner man, and exerts there his marvellous energy. He keeps Himself unseen, and focuses all our thought on the Lord Jesus, as light is sometimes made to fall on some beautiful face which attracts the observer's entire attention. Thus it happens that though the brunt of the inner war is borne by the Spirit (Gal. 5: 17), yet the believer is occupied with Jesus, appealing to Him in the conflict, and softly breathing his name as a talisman of victory. Yet why do we need to distinguish thus, when They are One?

The power of the Holy Ghost works through our faith. —God will do all that we can trust Him to do ; but He does not pledge Himself to work independently of our faith. When faith is in strong and blessed exercise, there is no limit to its possibilities, because it taps the reservoirs of Omnipotence, and opens the sluice-gates, so that all God's power begins to flow into the soul. Our faith is

24

the means of our receptivity; the straits through which the ocean of Divine fullness pours its tides.

But if our faith be meagre and struggling, we cannot expect mighty deliverances. Smite but thrice upon the ground, and Syria will still defy you (2 Kings 13:19). If you do not expect that God is able to keep you, do not be surprised if you are not kept. According to your faith, or unbelief, so will it be done to you.

Would you realise God's keeping grace? Give yourself entirely up to Him, renouncing all trust in yourself, and all connection with evil. Choose definitely and for ever the lot of the cross of Jesus. And then trust Jesus to keep you. Whenever temptation approaches, look up, and say, "Jesus, I trust Thy keeping power." Ask the Holy Spirit to keep you so constantly in this attitude that it may become the habit of your soul to look to Jesus when temptation assails. Trust Him to keep you trusting. Nourish your faith by devout meditation on the promises of God. Do not look at your weakness or your foes, but at the mighty bulwarks of God's salvation, which He has appointed. "The Lord is Thy Keeper." Hear his gracious words, and hide them in your heart: "I the Lord do keep it; I will water it every moment: lest any hurt it, I will keep it night and day." Surely it were the height of blasphemy to affirm that the Almighty is not able, or willing, to keep the soul that trusts Him. Only man would shake the fugitive dove out of his bosom to the hawk!

Thus will you await the consummation of your salvation, which shall be yours at the coming of the Lord. Already it is finished and prepared; but it waits to be revealed. And when, amid the breaking light and exuberant gladness of perfect deliverance, you review the pathway by which you have come, you will better realise your indebtedness to his wondrous grace, in keeping that which you committed to Him against that day.

4

FOR THOSE IN HEAVINESS

"In heaviness through manifold temptations: that the trial of your faith, being much more precious than of gold that perisheth, though it be tried with fire, might be found unto praise and honour and glory at the appearing of Jesus Christ."—1 PETER 1:6, 7.

Heaviness! "He began to be sorrowful, and very heavy." It was only through the darkness of that garden that He could pass upward to the glory of the Resurrection morn. And it is impossible to depict the condition of deep human suffering more accurately than by the words, "in heaviness." As the leaves of the laurel are pressed to the earth by the weight of a thunder shower, so are souls made heavy "by manifold temptations."

Temptation here is equivalent to trial. In other days the same word was used indiscriminately of the *testings,* which befall the saints, on the part of God and of the devil. The one, that we may know ourselves as He knows us, and that the first small germs of good which He has implanted may develop by use into strong and beautiful maturity. The other, that the evil within us may be made manifest, and hurried into such action as will cast down our hopes, and sow the seeds of future indulgence. The motive of God's testings is benevolence, that we may be nobler, sweeter, riper. The motive of Satan's is malignity, that we may be hastened down the sliding-scale of sin. Thus God is said in the Scriptures to tempt men, and yet not to tempt them (Gen. 22:1; James 1:13). He tests and tries them, but never allures them into evil.

In our desire to distinguish between these two methods of testing, we for the most part employ different words, using *trial of the divinely-ordered discipline of life,* and *temptation* of the attacks of the great enemy of our souls. And, therefore, it is more appropriate to modern usage to speak of being in heaviness "through manifold trials."

This is also suggested by the Revised Version. (*See also* James 1:2).

"Manifold trials."—In this Epistle, as in a mirror, we can see reflected the dark shadows which were gathering over these scattered saints. Buffeted for doing well; reviled and suffering; exposed to railing and terror; evil spoken of; tried in a fiery trial; partakers of Christ's sufferings; reproached for the name of Christ; judgment beginning at the house of God; experiencing the same afflictions as fell to the lot of brethren throughout the world: such are some of the hints given throughout this Epistle of the sources of their manifold trials. To "suffer as a Christian" (4:16), meant the loss of business, repute, and home; desertion by parents, children, and friends; misrepresentation, hatred, and even death. The new convert became the target for every weapon, hurled from any quarter.

For ourselves, trials come generally from three sources: those brought on us by others; those caused by our own sins, mistakes, and indiscretions; and those sent to us directly from God, our Father. And beneath this various pressure, what wonder that the heart is bowed down! How apt was the summons of Jesus to the *heavy-laden*; and how incessant the great procession of such passing down into the Vale of Tears, at the end of which stands his cross, behind which the light of morning is breaking!

The Apostle does not blame this heaviness.—The Stoic scorns to shed a tear: the Christian is not forbidden to weep; yea, he follows the best example in letting his tears have free course. We must not despise the chastening of the Lord, any more than we should faint under it. Strong crying and tears befit sons who are learning obedience by suffering. The soul may be dumb with excessive grief, as the shearer's scissors pass over the quivering flesh; or, when the heart is on the point of breaking beneath the meeting surges of trial, the sufferer may seek relief by crying out with a loud voice.

But there is something even better. They say that springs of sweet fresh water well up amid the brine of salt seas; that the fairest Alpine flowers bloom in the wildest and most rugged mountain passes; that the noblest psalms were the outcome of the profoundest agony of soul. Be it so. And thus amid manifold trials souls which love God will find reasons for bounding, leaping joy. Though deep call to deep, yet the Lord's song will be heard in silver cadence through the night. And it is possible in the darkest hour that ever swept a human life to bless the God and Father of our Lord Jesus Christ. Have your learnt this lesson yet? Not simply to endure God's will; nor only to choose it; nor only to trust it—but to rejoice in it with joy unspeakable and full of glory.

Of such joy there are two sources: first, the understanding of the nature and meaning of trial; second, the soul's love and faith in its unseen Lord. There is enough in these two for unsullied and transcendent joy; in fact, we may question whether we ever truly drink of Christ's joy, till all other sources of joy are eliminated by earthly sorrow, and we are driven to seek that joyous blessedness which no earthly sun can wither and no winter freeze (Heb. 3: 17—19).

I. THE NATURE AND MEANING OF TRIAL.—*Trial is here compared to fire*; that subtle element, which is capable of inflicting such exquisite torture on our seared and agonized flesh; which cannot endure the least taint or remnant of impurity, but wraps its arms around objects committed to it with eager intensity to set them free and make them pure; which is careless of agony, if only its passionate yearning may be satisfied; which lays hold of things more material than itself, loosening their texture, snapping their fetters, and bearing them upwards in its heaven-aspiring energy. What better emblem could there be for God, and for those trials which He permits or sends, and in the heart of which He is to be found? Ah, the agony of suffering is keen to bear—when friends forsake, and enemies reproach, and the work of years is suddenly shattered, and the soul is stung with pain and shame and ingratitude, with disappointment and bereavement: such suffering is to the soul what fire is to the flesh.

(1) *But this fire is a refiner's fire.*—The reference is evident. And we are taken back to an olden prophecy, from which we learn that when the Lord comes to his temple, He sits as a refiner beside the crucible (Mal. 3:3). We may well take the shoes from off our feet, when we enter the chamber of some tried Christian, for certainly the Lord is there.

It is He who permits the trial.—The evil thing may originate in the malignity of a Judas; but by the time it reaches us it has become the cup which our Father has given us to drink. The waster may purpose his own law-

28

less and destructive work; but he cannot go an inch beyond the determinate counsel and foreknowledge of God. Satan himself must ask permission ere he touches a hair of the patriarch's head (Job 1:8—12). The point up to which we may be tested is fixed by consummate wisdom. The weapon may hurt and the fire sting; but they are in the hands which redeemed us. Nothing can befall us without God's permission, and his permissions are his appointments. We cannot be the sport of blind fate or chance; for in trial we are still in the hands of the Divine Saviour.

It is He who superintends the trial.—No earthly friend may be near; but in every furnace there is One like the Son of Man. In every flood of high waters He stands beside us—staying the heart with promises, instilling words of faith and hope, recalling the blessed past, pointing to the radiant future, hushing fear, as once He stilled the dismay of his disciples on the lake: such is the ministry of Jesus. And as the sufferer looks back on the trial, he says, "I never felt Him so near before; and if it had not been for what He was to me, I could never have lived through it."

It is He who watches the progress of the trial.—No mother bending over her suffering child is more solicitous than is He—suiting the trial to your strength—keeping his finger on your pulse so as to stay the flame when the heart begins to flutter—only too eager to see the scum pass off, and his own face reflected from the face of the molten metal.

Happy would it be for us if, instead of looking at our trials, we would look away to his face, only eager to understand his meaning, and to learn his intended lesson, so that as the outward man perishes, the inward man may be renewed day after day. Whilst the marble wastes beneath the sculptor's hand, the image grows; so should each loss in our state or circumstance have a corresponding gain in spiritual conformity to Christ.

(2) *Trial is only for a season.*—"Now for a season, ye are in heaviness" (*ver.* 6). The great Husbandman is not always threshing. The showers soon pass. Weeping may only tarry for the few hours of the short summer night: it must be gone at daybreak. Our light affliction is but for a moment.

There is a subtle distinction here between the most precious and enduring of material substances and the faith of the Christian soul. "Gold that perisheth" (*ver.* 7).

29

Gold outlasts carved wood, and the potter's art, and most things else. It may be attenuated and worn by long use, yet will it survive the gentle hand on which it has spoken of unending love for half a century. Yet gold will eventually wear out. But there is that in each of us which cannot perish. The mere accident of death cannot affect it, nor the flight of time, nor the descent of all created things into the gulf of oblivion. It is eternal as the God who inspired it. And compared to that boundless existence which is its birthright, how paltry and insignificant do the longest trials appear, though they have lain for many years on the soul and life! Judged by the measureless span of eternity, they are but for a season, and will pass as completely from memory as the clouds of early morning before the meridian glory of a long summer day.

(3) *Trial is for a purpose.*—"It needs be." There is nothing harder to bear than the apparent aimlessness of sorrow. A new interest comes into the monotony of prison-discipline as soon as the convicts feel that their toils are achieving some positive result. And when no purpose seems secured by our sufferings or toils, hope dies.

With the Christian there is no fear of this. There is a utility in every trial. It is intended to reveal the secrets of our hearts; to humble us and prove us; to winnow us as corn is shaken in a sieve; to detach us from the earthly and visible; to create in us an eager desire for the realities which can alone quench our cravings and endure for ever. We must not look on trial as punishment for the past; because all penalty has been borne for us by our Redeemer. But each trial points to the future, and is intended to make us partakers of his holiness, and to work in us the peaceable fruit of righteousness. The very fact of trial proves that there is something in us very precious to our Lord: else He would not spend so much pains and time on us. "We do not prune brambles, or cast stones into the crucible, or plough the sea-sands."[1] And Christ would not test us if He did not see the precious ore of faith mingled in the rocky matrix of our nature; and it is to bring this out into purity and beauty that He forces us through the fiery ordeal. Be patient, O sufferer: He must love you, or He would not chasten you; you must be his, or He would not take such pains with you; you must be capable of some high service which can only be secured through pain, or He would not plunge you into the refining fires. You must be able to

30

bear the fire, or He would not pass you through it (Num. 31:23).

The result will more than compensate us.—"Found unto praise, and honour, and glory, at the appearing of Jesus Christ." The gold is well repaid for the fires when it encircles the monarch's brow; the diamond for the lapidary's wheel when it glistens on the neck of beauty. And we shall be more than recompensed for all our trials, when we see how they wrought out the far more exceeding and eternal weight of glory. To have one word of God's commendation; to be honoured before the holy angels; to be glorified in Christ, so as to be better able to flash back his glory on Himself—ah! this will more than repay for all. Let us live more constantly in that future, under the powers of the world to come!—as soldiers solace themselves in the arduous campaign by talking over their watchfires of the welcome and rewards which will greet them on their return. "Now they do it to receive a corruptible crown, but we an incorruptible" (1 Cor. 9:25). All the blessings which accrue through trial are only possible to us, however, when the heart meekly accepts it from the hand of God, and *opens to the operation of the Holy Spirit*. Trial alone may harden, as the fire which softens wax hardens clay to bricks. But when trial is accompanied with the gracious influences of the Holy Spirit, it is as precious oil that does not break the head (Psa. 141:5).

See how much God thinks of faith.—It is priceless in his esteem. What gold is to the miser, faith is to God. It is the root of all other grace, the germ of the saintly life, the key to the Divine storehouse, the foot of the heavenly ladder, the earthward pier of the arch that bridges the abyss between the unseen and the seen. To make it strong in one poor heart is a matter of extreme value in his sight. And since it can only grow strong by use, and exercise, and strain, be not surprised if He exposes you to discipline, graduated according to your power, but becoming ever severer, until beneath his gracious tuition the faith, which once shivered at sight of the shallows, will plunge fearlessly into the deep, and do business in mighty waters,

¹ Charles Stanford.

5

CHRIST UNSEEN, BUT LOVED

*"Whom, having not seen, ye love; in whom, though
now ye see Him not, yet believing, ye rejoice with joy
unspeakable and full of glory: receiving the end of your
faith, even the salvation of your souls."*—1 PETER 1:8, 9.

The sixth verse begins, and the eight ends, with a Greek
word expressive of leaping, bounding joy.[1] It is strange
that such a word should be used of the feelings experienced
by handfuls of scattered saints over whom the dark
thunder-clouds of persecution were beginning to gather
heavily. And yet it is not strange when we study the
sources of that joy, which are included within these golden
brackets, the first of which we considered in our previous chapter. Is there not joy in the thought that trial
is the refiner's fire, sharp but salutary—the necessary
preparation for results of immeasurable blessedness? And
is there not yet deeper cause for joy, triumphant and
exulting, in the relation into which we have been brought
with Jesus Christ our Lord?

Yes, the iron may hiss, and the fire sting; friends may
desert, and foes may threaten; the cold waters may creep
up around our person, and the shadows of the dark
valley fling themselves between us and the sunshine; nevertheless, whatever be the nature or severity of our manifold trials, it shall be enough for us to know that they
are working out the results of untold glory, and that
nothing can break that holy and blessed personal relationship into which we have entered with Him whom
Bernard never tired of addressing as *Jesus Master*.

Jesus, then, is the Heart and Centre of these burning
words; words which recall the thrice-repeated question of
the Lake of Galilee, *Lovest thou Me?* and the never-to-
be-forgotten beatitude of the upper chamber, *Blessed
are they that have not seen, and yet have believed!* (John
20:29). And is not this text an epitome of Christianity?
What makes us Christians except that we believe in and

love Him whose receding form was veiled by the chariot-cloud that swept beneath Him as He passed home to heaven? We may accept and appreciate the words of many of the world's great thinkers, whilst we concern ourselves but little with the men themselves; but we may not do this with the words of Christ, and still be Christians. We cannot take his words, and ignore Him. Christianity is the personal relationship of the soul to Christ. Begin, not with his words, but with Himself; and when you possess Him, you cannot fail of having all He said, and did, and is, and will be, world without end.

I. AN UNSEEN CHRIST—A POSSIBLE HINDERANCE TO EXULTING JOY.—"Not having seen"; "Now ye see Him not." To a superficial thinker this privation of a personal vision of Jesus might be deemed sufficient to put all after-ages on a lower platform than that glad first one which looked upon his face—the face which reflected the moods of his tranquil and holy nature; which lit up homes of sorrow and lives of despair with the radiance of hope; which attracted little children to his embrace; and which often shone with the gleam of celestial communications, glancing between Him and God. Surely not to have seen it might count as an irreparable loss!

An old divine said that he wished he could have seen three things—Rome in her glory; Paul preaching at Athens; and Christ in the body. And it was because of their desire to satisfy themselves, and to meet this great longing, that the great painters of Christendom covered the walls of picture galleries with conceptions of the face of Jesus. Crowds have stood transfixed and touched before these masterpieces of art. But who has not turned from the very noblest of them with a sigh of dissatisfaction, and a secret conviction that even if the sublimest feature were to be taken out of each separate picture and all combined into one, the face so composed must still fall infinitely short of that in which Deity and humanity met, and shone, and wept, and loved. We shall never see anything worthy of that face till we see Him as He is. "They shall see his face," and "the glory of God in the face of Jesus Christ" (Rev. 22:4; 2 Cor. 4:6).

But is there not hardship and irreparable loss in this? Not so. He can be nearer, dearer to us to-day, than if those old blessed days in which He walked with his disciples over the hills of Galilee, or fell asleep in the stern of Peter's boat, had been drawn out like a golden thread

33

throughout the centuries. We could not have always had Him then. Domestic duties; the needs of the world; the requirements of food, or business, or sleep—must have taken us from his side. Or, at the best, we could only have known Him as part of a great multitude, all of whom would have been equally eager to possess Him for themselves. In the press of saints and apostles we must have necessarily occupied the outer rim of the vast crowd, and been satisfied with a transient glimpse, or with such beams as those which travel from our sun to Uranus, on the extreme limits of our system. And amid it all, there might have been a strong temptation to such earthly, sensuous love as made the woman of the crowd exclaim, "Blessed is she that bare thee, and the breasts which thou has sucked;" expressions which He corrected by immediately recalling the thoughts of the crowd to the greater blessedness of those who "hear the word of God, and keep it" (Luke 11:28).

If we had seen Him once, or might see Him still, our joy would have been dashed with the pain of losing Him; of intermittent fellowship; or of the necessity of sharing Him with others. It would have been too deeply-rooted in the outward and physical. It would have languished when manifold trials intercepted its vision. It could never have possessed that vigour; that independence of circumstances; that power to defy imprisonment, solitude, and desertion; that buoyant and heavenward ardour—which indicate that its temper is celestial, its nature Spirit-given. Therefore the invisibility of Jesus, which might have seemed inimical to our joy, so far from being so, is rather a condition of its existence in the soul; and for this reason, that as a spiritual presence our dear Lord can be more to us and more with us, than if He had lingered ever on our earth. Did He not therefore say Himself, "It is expedient for you that I go away"? Christ dwelling in our heart by the Spirit, with us, around us, in us, is infinitely more than He could have been to us, though, like Peter, James, and John, we had been the chosen companions of His earthly life.

II. TWO LINKS UNITE US TO THE UNSEEN LORD.—"Ye love." "Believing" (8). It is hard to say which is first or chief. We cannot love without believing, nor can we believe without loving. Faith is light; and love is heat. Where one enters, the other follows. Woven in the texture of each of heaven's sunbeams, we cannot have one

34

without the other; and our joy will be in direct proportion to the presence of these twin celestial sisters in our souls.

(1) AS TO LOVE.—No man is a Christian who does not love the Lord Jesus. "If any man love not the Lord Jesus Christ, let him be anathema" (1 Cor. 16: 22). This is the touchstone of trial for each one of us; not what we profess or say, but whether we love, and how much. But let us remember that *love reveals itself differently* according to that aspect of Christ's person or work on which the Spirit has fixed the beholder's eye. In some, conscious of a great deliverance, it takes the form of *gratitude*. In others, smitten with the beauty of his character, of *complacency*. In others, again, pre-occupied with his claims, of reverential *devotion to his service*. The symptoms of its presence are manifold. Sometimes adoring silence; at others irrepressible tears; or the sudden burning of the cheek; or unostentatious acts of mercy; or steadfastness in confessing Him at all costs. Love betrays itself, whether it fetches water from the well of Bethlehem at peril of life, or comes with precious spikenard to anoint the dear body of the dead.

Those that love Christ most, often accuse themselves of not loving Him. Their love so conceives of Him that He seems deserving of something infinitely better than they can give. They love Him so much, that they would be almost prepared to make way for any who could love Him better; and yet to stand aside would be agony. Let such take heart! He who knows all things, knows how much they love. And, after all, love is measured, not by feelings, or sighs, or tears, but by acts. You love Christ by just as much as you are prepared to do, or suffer, or give up for Him.

How may we love Christ more?—Spend much time alone in contemplating what He has done for you; and what He is, as the "chiefest among ten thousand" and the "altogether lovely." Stir the inner fire by means of memory; and let hope pile on it the fuel of promise till it begin to blaze. Cultivate the habit of speaking aloud to Him, in an empty chamber, or a lonely walk, until He be interlaced in the tiniest episodes of existence. Open your heart to the entrance of the Holy Spirit, shedding abroad the love of God in the heart, and gathering the rays of that love into a burning focus, so that you may love God back with love which has come from his heart into yours. And, very specially, accustom yourself to do, for the sake of his dear love, many things which cost you self-sacrifice and effort. As we show love to others we understand his love to ourselves. "Every one that loveth is born of God, and knoweth God. He that loveth not knoweth not God; for God is love" (1 John 4: 7, 8).

The key to the knowledge of the love of Jesus is not in singing rapturous hymns, nor in seeking to arouse intense emotion; but in quietly doing daily deeds of self-denial for His sake. And surely this is the way to sow ourselves as corns of wheat in the ground (John 12: 24); whilst he measures the least act of love, not by the magnitude of the deed itself, but by the strength of the love which prompts it. It is astonishing how quickly we graduate in the school of love, when we begin to put in practice all we know.

(2) AS TO FAITH.—Who is there of us that does not often cry with the disciples: "Lord, increase our faith!"? Certain it is that increased faith would mean increased joy. But are we all prepared to use the means within our reach for obtaining this increased faith? The germ of faith is the creative gift of God; but its nurture and culture lie with us, by the grace of the Holy Spirit.

The conditions of its growth are these:—There must be, *first,* the putting away from the heart and life of all known evil and inconsistency. The reason for much of the weak faith around is to be found in the permission of forbidden and questionable things, which clog and oppress the soul. These are the bird-lime on the soul's wings—the hood on the inner vision. *Next,* there must be time given for quiet musing over the statements and promises of the Word of God, till they assume a definite shape as eternal facts. *Lastly,* there must be habitual obedience to every known duty; so that, as the will of God is revealed, it shall be instantly embodied in action; and this, notwithstanding any difficulty that may line the path. Where these rules are observed, faith will grow exceedingly, and will make the unseen Saviour "a living bright reality" to the soul which yearns for a hand that can never fail, a heart that can never cease to throb.

III. THE RESULTING JOY.—*Is there not joy in love* when a barrier is broken down which had estranged for years; when confession is made and forgiveness is granted; when heart flows to heart; when the golden key of love unlocks the choicest and most sacred treasures? To know

36

that since we love Christ, we must have been loved; that we are loved with a love which will never let us go, but which will cling to us through life and death and eternal ages, not for anything good or worthy in us, but because of its own sweet will and choice; to be persuaded that nothing, not even our failures and inconsistencies, can separate us from the love of Christ—this, surely, must thrill us with joy, however great and manifold may be the trials through which we are called to pass.

Is there not joy in faith?—"Think with what joy the long-imprisoned debtor, drowned in debt, receives a full discharge and his liberty; or a condemned malefactor the news of his pardon—and this will somewhat resemble it, and yet fall far short of the joy which faith imparts, by bringing Christ into the soul and forgiveness of sins in Him. Nor is this all, for the believing soul is not only a debtor acquitted, but enriched besides with a new and great estate, having the right to the unsearchable riches of Christ, to the favour of God, and to the dignity of his child."

Such joy is unspeakable.—There are times of high tide in the believer's soul, when he dare not speak. Words seem superfluous and empty. The tides overflow their banks, and pour their volume in unspoken admiration into the heart of God.

And full of glory.—It is of the same substance, if not of the same bulk and weight, as the glory which awaits us on the other side. There are moments of heaven upon earth; prelibations of the river of life; stray notes of the angel choruses; Eschol grapes from the vineyards of the land of promise; flowers from the parterres of Paradise. Oh for more of heaven on the way to heaven! A prayer which we may almost answer for ourselves by seeking more of Him who is Himself the heaven of heaven; and so adopting Bengel's motto: "Christ in the heart; heaven in the heart; the heart in heaven."

[1] $\dot{\alpha}\gamma\alpha\lambda\lambda\iota$ ω—to rejoice exceedingly.

6

THE SUFFERINGS AND GLORIES OF CHRIST

"Concerning which salvation the prophets sought and searched diligently, who prophesied of the grace that should come unto you: searching what time or what manner of time the Spirit of Christ which was in them did point unto when it testified beforehand the sufferings of Christ, and the glories that should follow them. To whom it was revealed, that not unto themselves, but unto you, did they minister these things, which now have been announced unto you through them that preached the gospel unto you by the Holy Ghost sent forth from heaven; which things angels desire to look into."—1 PETER 1:10—12 (R.V.).

Thirty years, full of varied absorbing interest, had well-nigh passed away since Peter—amid the gloom of Gethsemane; or as one of the little crowd of servants in the high priest's hall; or as a heartbroken spectator on the outer rim of the crowd—had been an eyewitness of the sufferings of Christ; sufferings from the endurance of which he had done his utmost to dissuade his Master. But they were as fresh as though they had been borne but yesterday, like the blood-red of the sandstone rocks, which remains as vivid as on the morning of creation, though thousands of autumns have strewn them with the fading hues of nature's many-coloured dress. Throughout the Epistle there is repeated reference to the sufferings which culminated at Calvary. But how different is the tone in which the Apostle alludes to them! A vast change has passed over him since, on the eve of the Transfiguration, he said: "This shall not be unto Thee." That which had aroused his strongest protestation is now better understood, and has become the theme of his tenderest love (*comp.* Matt. 16:22 with 1 Pet. 1:11; 2:21, 23; 3:18; 4:1, 13; 5:1).

By those sufferings, our salvation has been achieved. —SALVATION is a great word. And some glimpses of the width of its contents are discovered in the Apostle's three-fold use of it here (verses 5, 9, 10). It is so great and glorious that the saintliest souls cannot in this world fully realise all its blessedness. It will only be revealed "in the last time" (5), because it includes the deliverance of our bodies from the bondage of corruption, and their trans-figuration into the likeness of the body of Christ's glory; a result which cannot be attained till the second coming of the Lord. Moreover, "salvation" includes something more than deliverance from the penalty due to sin, to which its meaning is so often limited. It is SALVATION FOR SOULS (ver. 9)—that is: it not only makes them safe—but also sound, healthy, wholesome, and whole; breathing into them the very nature of God; and replacing corruption with the life of the eternal world. Well may the Apostle find an equivalent for such a salvation, cov-ering as it does our entire nature, in the sweet old word GRACE. Who shall estimate the "grace" that has come to us in the coming of such a salvation as this? (ver. 10).

On this "salvation" we must not linger longer now, fascinating though the theme must be to those who owe all to it, both in this life and the next. But, as we pass from it, we ask our readers to inquire whether they have experienced it, not only as a *past* act, breaking the entail of a deserved penalty; or as a *future* act, uniting spot-less soul and stainless body in the presence of the King; but as a living *present* enjoyment, securing for them daily, hourly, victory over known sin, whether suggested from within or by the malevolence of our great spiritual foe.

The sufferings of Christ, then, must engage our thought, and under a peculiar aspect.—In a picture of the cruci-fixion, by a great modern painter, we stand behind the cross, not seeing the sufferer, but only the shadows of three crosses falling down the hill-slope, the central one being the deepest and broadest of the three. But the faces of those passing by, or standing near, are toward us, and are filled with looks which tell the story of the tragedy in a way which the minutest delineation of horrors could never have done. So we are studying the sufferings of Christ in their effect on the witness of the Spirit; the testimony of the prophets; the preaching of the Apostles; and the rapt gaze of the angels.

1. THE WITNESS OF THE SPIRIT—"It testified before-hand the sufferings of Christ." The name here given to the Holy Spirit is very significant. He is called *the Spirit*

of Christ. One as He is with the Father and the Son in the mystery of the Holy Trinity, and proceeding as a stream of holy influence from their common throne, yet He bends all his influence to reveal and glorify our blessed Lord. In Himself He is ineffably holy, loving, mighty—whom to know is everlasting blessedness. And yet, with marvellous and divine unobtrusiveness, He withdraws Himself from our notice, only anxious to focus all attention and interest on the Christ (John 16:13—15).

Until Jesus was glorified, the Spirit was not fully given (John 7:39)—not poured out freely upon all, as afterwards at Pentecost (Acts 2:17), but in measure, and occasionally (*comp.* Judges 13:25). Even before the Incarnation, He broke out in witness to the coming Saviour, and with irrepressible love gave testimony to Jesus; as when the voice of the Father refused to be longer bound by the restraints of a self-imposed silence, but broke out in benediction after the baptism of the Son in the waters of Jordan.

Nor is it wonderful that the Spirit's testimony pointed in the direction of Christ's sufferings. The offering up of Christ in death is said to have been through the "Eternal Spirit" (Heb. 9:14). It was an act, in which the Trinity as a whole participated. It was the crystalisation in the concrete of an eternal thought in the counsel and purpose of God (Rev. 13:8). It was probably the most stupendous event in the existence of the Blessed God. How, then, can we wonder at the Holy Spirit anticipating the discoveries of time, and giving premonitory hints and signs, and anticipations of the sufferings of the cross? It is surely a mistake, then, for us to make so little, in meditation and in ministry, of that which is the supreme point of interest to the Spirit of Christ in the work of the Saviour upon our world! The emphasis that He lays on the sufferings of Christ, like the word *seach* on a cairn, might indicate what inestimable treasures lie beneath.

And if the Blessed Spirit dwell so lovingly and gladly on the sufferings, how much more on the glories of the Lord! The Apostle laid the emphasis there when he said, "Yea, rather that was raised from the dead" (Rom. 8:34, R.V.). And deservedly, because the glories are the crown and flower and fruit of the sufferings; the attestation of his Deity; the Divine imprimatur on his work; the reward for the travail of his soul. Stay, my soul, to recount the glories, one by one, of the Resurrection morning; the Ascension mount; the triumphal procession through all ranks of being; the session at the right hand of God; the Second Advent; and the Millennial Reign.

II. THE BURDEN OF THE GOODLY FELLOWSHIP OF PROPHETS. —From the age of Samuel these men appear. Very zealous for the Lord of Hosts, and full of the loftiest patriotism, they fulfilled a great ministry to their times, serving the same purpose as the Tribunes of the People in ancient Rome, and the public press to-day. They stood up before kings for the rights of the people, as they stood up before the people for the rights of God. Nathan before David; Elijah before Ahab; Isaiah before Ahaz; Jeremiah before Zedekiah; John before Herod.

With us, the word "Prophet" looks out on the future, penetrating its veil; but in the original it means "bubbling up," as when the Psalmist said that his heart was bubbling up with good matter (Psa. 45:1), like springs forcing their way out into the desert waste, making it smile and bloom. Nevertheless, in their public utterances, which were primarily addressed to men of their time, there were depths of meaning, references, and anticipations, which demanded a fuller realisation than could be found in a series of national events, however momentous.

It was the distinguishing mark of the Jews, that, unlike other nations, their golden age lay before them as a radiant goal, and that their greatest Hero was not their father, but his remote Descendant. Expectation stooped forward, intent on catching the first foot-fall of the coming King, who should gather up and satisfy the loftiest hopes. Of these expectations and hopes the prophets were the chief exponents. But this would not have sufficed to explain the fulness and minuteness of detail which characterise their words. There was an element present which can be accounted for by no earthly or human prescience. These holy men spake from God, being moved by the Holy Ghost (2 Pet. 1:21, R.V.).

The Spirit of Christ was in them.—First, He was in them as the Spirit of Revelation, communicating truths which they could not have foreseen or discovered; truths which even baffled their understanding after they had received them. Next, He was in them as the Spirit of inspiration, affording spiritual aid in promulgating truth; so that the Bible contains God's truth stated in human words, which nevertheless give an adequate and sufficient statement of the Divine intention and purpose.

And it is easy, therefore, to understand that the burden

41

of their words would be the same as that which engrossed the blessed Spirit. Through them He testified of the sufferings and the glory. The crimson cord of Calvary surrounds every window in the sacred book. In each voice there is the wail of the cross and the hallelujah of ressurection. Moses and Elias speak of the decease (*the exode*) to be accomplished. And thus, as the Master talked with the two disciples on the road to Emmaus, He was able to expound to them in all the Scriptures that Christ ought to suffer and to enter into his glory (Luke 24:26, 27, 46). Well, too, might Paul reason at Thessalonica for three whole Sabbath days, opening and alleging that Christ must needs have suffered, and risen again from the dead (Acts 17:3).

But though the prophets spake of these things, they but imperfectly understood them. They searched into the very matters of which they were made the organs and channels. Like Daniel, they "heard, but understood not" (Dan. 12:8). They could not interpret the hieroglyphs of the dates, nor foresee the mystery and glory of the coming days. And often were the saintliest Jews puzzled at the marvellous conjunction of death with life; of travail with triumph; of darkness with light—on the pages of their prophetic books.

They had to content themselves with ministering to us; and they have performed a very efficient service: because the simplest believer has now an irrefragable testimony to the Divine truthfulness of Scripture, in being able to compare the predictions of the Old Testament with their fulfilment in the New, fitting each other as the two sides of a tally, or as a key and lock. There is no proof of the Divine authority of the Bible greater than this.

III. THE PREACHING OF THE APOSTLES was full of the same theme (ver. 12). The Gospel which they announced was the tidings of the death and resurrection of their Lord. They preached Jesus Christ, and Him crucified. They gloried above all things in the cross. It was a matter of perfect indifference that to the Jews it was a stumbling-block, and to the Greeks foolishness: the Apostles persisted in declaring that God had made that same Jesus, whom men had crucified, both Lord and Christ (Acts 2:36; 4:10).

And with such preaching the Holy Ghost was able to co-operate—The Apostles preached in the power of the

Spirit. The Spirit is said in this verse to have announced these things through them. It was a theme which attracted all his tenderest, mightiest interest. He who spake in and with the Apostles, working powerfully on human hearts by their ministry. And so their preaching, if not with enticing words of man's wisdom, was in demonstration of the Spirit and of power. Yes, and if only men will still dare to preach the doctrine of the cross, they will find again, other things being equal, that results will accrue which bear the Divine hallmark.

IV. THE THEME OF THE ANGELS is the same blessed topic. They desire to "look into" these things. They bend aside, as did the cherubim over the mercy-seat, where these truths were set forth in the sprinkled blood. They may have held high debate about the full import of the Saviour's death; but though they cannot penetrate all its mysterious depths, yet they set to music all they know, crying, "Worthy the Lamb that was slain!" The cross attracts the keenest interest of bright celestial spirits.

It may be that those sufferings have brought angels nearer God; but in any case, they have given deep and marvellous glimpses into his heart; such as else could never have come to them. Rightly they are lost in admiration and praise.

If the angels, with their opportunities of knowledge, find ever fresh fields of interest and investigation in the sufferings of Christ and the glories that are to follow, how little do the wisest of us know of them! We are but ankle-deep at the furthest in this fathomless ocean. We are still at the alphabet—the primer of knowledge.

But surely enough has been said to invest the Saviour's sufferings with new interest, as we turn to them again to find heights, depths, lengths, and breadths of meaning, which have engaged and baffled prophets and kings, angels and saints.

7

"YE SHALL BE HOLY"

"Wherefore girding up the loins of your mind, be sober and set your hope perfectly on the grace that is to be brought unto you at the revelation of Jesus Christ; as children of obedience, not fashioning yourselves according to your former lusts in the time of your ignorance: but like as He which called you is holy, be ye yourselves also holy in all manner of living; because it is written, Ye shall be holy; for I am holy. And if ye call on Him as Father, who without respect of persons judgeth according to each man's work, pass the time of your sojourning in fear."—1 PETER 1: 13—17 (R.V.).

The "wherefore" with which this paragraph opens gathers up the premises of the preceding verses, and uses them as a massive platform of solid masonry on which to erect the battery of appeal to which the Apostle now addresses himself. Because our destiny is what it is; because Jesus Christ is what He is; because our salvation has been the theme of prophets, apostles, martyrs, angels; *therefore* . . .

And the *aim of his appeal is Holiness.*—"Be ye yourselves also holy in all manner of living." The cry for HOLINESS rings though the Bible. It is the keynote of Leviticus, from which this quotation is made (*comp.* ver. 16 with Lev. 11:44; 19:2; 20:7 and 26, &c.): and it is equally the supreme demand of the New Testament. In point of fact, all the wondrous machinery of redemption, from the distant choice of eternity to the descent of the Holy Spirit on the Day of Pentecost, has had this for its purpose, that we, who have been the subjects of the grace of the Persons of the Eternal Trinity, should resemble them in the holiness which is the perpetual burden of heaven's rapturous minstrelsy—that song which was heard by the evangelic prophet Isaiah from the Temple courts, in the year that King Uzziah died; but which was still unfinished when the beloved Apostle

John detected it amid the break of the Ægean Sea around the lone island of his banishment; and which will never cease, world without end: "Holy, holy, holy, is the Lord God the Almighty" (Isa. 6:3 ; Rev. 4:8).

Holiness is the property of God alone.—It is the totality of the Divine attributes; the sum of the Eternal and Infinite Being of God-head; the essence of Deity; the chord made by the harmonious blending of Divine qualities; the beam woven from the many colours of Divine perfections; the expression in a single term of all that goes to make up the moral nature of the great Spirit whom we call GOD. It is underived in its source; unlimited in its measure; insupportable in its naked and unveiled splendour by the eye of any creature which He has made. "Who is like unto Thee, O Lord glorious in holiness, fearful in praises, doing wonders?" (Exod. 15:11). No tongue then shall dare to challenge God's right to declare Himself as the Holy One of Israel, or to say in the words before us, "I am holy."

Such holiness is evidently possible to us.—See, the holy God has "called" us to it (*v.* 15). "God hath not called us to uncleanness, but to holiness" (1 Thess. 4:7). He "hath called us with a holy calling" (2 Tim. 1:9). All partakers of the heavenly calling are called "holy brethren" (Heb. 3:1). But God would not summon us to heights we could not scale, or to tasks we could not perform. His CALL involves two facts—first, that his holiness is within our reach; secondly, that He is prepared to supply all that is necessary to effect in us that to which He calls us. God is pledged to make us holy; or He will expose Himself to the mockery of his foes. But we need not fear for Him. He counted the cost before He issued his proclamation; and He is well able to finish that of which He laid the foundation in the great depths of Calvary (Luke 14:29, 30).

Nor is such holiness for saints and apostles alone; or only for the special golden days which visit most lives —days of feast and song and transfiguration. The Divine ideal is more comprehensive far. "Holy in all manner of living" (*v.* 15, R.V.). Zechariah foretold the time when the inscription on the high priest's mitre should be written even on the bells of the horses: "Holiness to the Lord." And it is God's will that that motto should be engraved on house bells, and office bells, and shop bells ; on dinner bells and factory bells ; so that in every department of our lives there may be sweet music made to life's great Lord. Holiness at every turn, and in every incident of our daily walk, like the golden tinkle which betrayed each movement of Israel's high priest (Exod. 28:33—35; Zech. 14:20, 21).

There is only one way of becoming holy, as God is: and it is the obvious one of opening the entire being to the all-pervading presence of the Holy One. None of us can acquire holiness apart from God. It dwells in God alone. Holiness is only possible as the soul's possession of God; nay, better still, as Gods' possession of the soul. It never can be inherent, or possessed apart from the Divine fullness, any more than a river can flow on if it is cut off from its fountain head. We are holy up to the measure in which we are God-possessed. The least holy man is he who shuts God up to the strictest confinement, and to the narrowest limits of his inner being; partitioning Him off from daily life by heavy curtains of neglect and unbelief. He is holier who more carefully denies self, and who seeks a larger measure of Divine indwelling. The holiest is the man who yields himself most completely to be influenced, swayed, possessed, inspired, by that Spirit who longs to make us to the fullest extent partakers of the Divine nature.

Wouldst thou be holier?—There is but one way. Thou must have more of God in thee. Holiness is the beauty of the Lord of hosts. Thou canst not separate the one from the other. To have *it* thou must have *Him.* Nor will it be hard to obtain either; for He longs to enter into thy being. Thy longing is the faint response of thy heart to his call. The power that works within is matched by the grace which can do for us exceeding abundantly above all that we ask or think. Man never desired so much of God as God desired of man. God's holiness has revealed itself in a human form in the person of Jesus Christ our Lord; and so it is as able as it is eager to enter human lives through that blessed Spirit who is pre-eminently the channel and medium by which we are filled up unto all the fullness of God. Ask thy heavenly Father for this Spirit. He is more eager to give Him than a father to give food to his hungry child. And, having asked, dare to believe that thou hast received, and "go in this thy might" (Jud. 6:14).

And this holiness will reveal itself in many ways.

I. THERE WILL BE THE PILGRIM ATTITUDE AND TEMPER.— Eastern fashions suggest the figure of *the girt loins.*

There the loose and flowing robes suit well the deliberate movements which the climate begets; but they would grievously hamper pilgrim, wrestler, or warrior. When the Israelites were momentarily expecting the summons for the Exodus, they stood with their loins girt around the tables on which the paschal lamb was smoking. Thus too did the prophet of fire gird himself for the swift courier-run before Ahab's chariot, from Carmel to Jezreel (1 Kings 18:46).

Our souls are clad with the flowing garments of various tastes, appetites, affections, and propensities, which hang loosely around us, constantly catching in the things of the world, and hindering us in the Christian race. We must not let them stream as they will—or we do so at our peril. Absalom rued the day when his luxuriant tresses floated behind him in the breeze. We must "gird up" the habits of our souls, and trim ourselves, so as to pass as quickly and easily as possible through the thorny jungle of the world.

Hold your spirit in a tight hand. Put a curb on appetite. Say "No" to luxurious pleasure-seeking. Curtail your expenditure on yourself. Do not spread yourself too widely. Watch eye and lip, thought and wish, lest any break from the containing cords of self-control. "Keep they heart with all thy diligence." Give Vanity Fair as little chance as possible, by passing swiftly and unostentatiously through.

Be sober!—Sobriety is a great word. It is constantly inculcated in the New Testament on elders, deacons, women, aged men, young men, and maidens. It means temperance, self-control, and a just estimate of one's self in the world. There are some who counterfeit it by assuming an austere and forbidding attitude, denouncing much that is innocent and natural, and looking severely on some who do not yield to their scruples. The truly sober man, on the other hand, moves freely through the world, strewn with beautiful and innocent things: using them without abuse, rejoicing in every good thing which the Lord God gives; but never allowing any of them to usurp too great an influence on his affections, or to tyrannise over his will.

When the heart is fully engaged with the Lord, his service, and love, and rewards, and welcome home at last, it can afford to look undazzled on many a captivating spectacle, and to turn from many a fascinating cup. The holy heart, filled to brimming with the presence

D
47

of God, is like a man who has been well banqueted, and who is therefore able to look calmly on the passionate heat with which starving men will fight with each other over offal.

Hope to the end.—"Set your hope perfectly" (R.V.). Go fearlessly as far as hope can go. Let her sit at her easel, painting her fairest pictures, or sing rapturously her most ecstatic lay: she cannot be disappointed. The "grace which is to be brought unto us" when the veiling clouds are rent, and the Lord Jesus is revealed from heaven, will far surpass all her imaginings. Hope is the lamp of the soul, passed down from saint to saint, as in the old Greek race, but destined to be eclipsed in the light which is to break ere long upon our spirits—the day of perfected redemption, of glorified creation, of a perfected church. The Revised Version reminds us that grace is being brought—it has started, and is already on its way.

II. THERE WILL BE THE OBEDIENCE OF CHILDREN (14).— Once the children of disobedience, we have been born again, and become children of obedience—a fair mother with noble offspring. Such, at least, is the literal rendering of the Greek. And what a marvellous difference at once comes over the lives of those who have passed through this change! They "no longer fashion themselves according to the former lusts."

Lust is natural inclination run wild, overlapping all restraint, and asserting its own imperious will. When we are yet in the darkness of nature, unillumined by the grace of God, these lusts fashion us. Beneath their touch we are moulded or *fashioned*, as clay by the potter's hand. Ignorant of the abominableness of sin, of its disastrous results, of its insidious growth, we yield to it until it becomes our tyrant and our ruin. Oh, the horror of the awakening, should we see the depths of this beetling precipice descending sheer beneath us to hell! When we no longer fashion ourselves according to the former lusts, but according to the will of God—that is *obedience*.

It is impossible to exaggerate the importance of this truth. Obedience is not holiness; holiness is the possession of the soul by God. But holiness always leads to obedience. And each time we obey, we receive into our natures a little more of the Divine nature. "If ye shall indeed obey my voice, ye shall be a holy nation unto Me." Do, then, whatever it is right to do. Forsake all which begins

48

and ends with self. Be not satisfied with prayer and desire, but DO. And thus there will come over your face and life more likeness to the Father of your spirits; and you will be holy.

How few Christian people seem to realise that obedience in trifles, in all things, to the will and law of Jesus, is the indispensable condition of life and joy and power. The obedient soul is the holy soul, penetrated and filled by the presence of God, and all aglow with light and love. Dear reader, resolve from this moment to live up to the margin of your light. Let this be your motto: "All that the Lord hath said will we do, and be obedient." Israel said this and failed utterly and shamefully; do you say it by the power of the Holy Spirit, and He shall make it gloriously possible.

III. THERE WILL BE A REVERENT ANTICIPATION OF THE FATHER'S AWARD (17).—God's children are to be judged, not at the great white throne, but at the judgment seat of Christ. (2 Cor. 5:10). That judgment will not decide our eternal destiny, because that has been settled before; but it will settle the rewards of our faithfulness or otherwise (Matt. 25:19; 1 Cor. 3:14).

There is a sense in which *that judgment is already in process,* and we are ever standing before the judgment bar. The Divine verdict is being pronounced perpetually on our actions, and hourly is manifesting itself in light or shadow.

But it is a *Father's judgment.* We call on Him as Father. Notice this reciprocity of calling. He called us; we call Him; his address to us as children begets our address to Him as Father. We need not dread his scrutiny—it is tender. He pities us as a father pities his children, knowing our frame, allowing for our weaknesses, and bearing with us with an infinite patience.

But for all that *it is impartial.* "Without respect of persons." Many years before, this had been revealed to the Apostle from heaven in a memorable vision, which affected his whole after-ministry (Acts 10:35). Not according to profession, or appearance, or any self-constituted importance, but according to what we do, are we being judged.

The holy soul realises this; and a great awe falls upon it and overshadows it—an awe not born of the fear which hath torment, but of love. It passes the time of its sojourning in fear. Not the fear of evil consequences to

itself, but the fear of grieving the Father; of bringing
a shadow over his face; of missing any manifestation
of his love and nearness to Himself, which may be granted
to the obedient child. Love casts out fear; but it also
begets it. There is nothing craven, or fretful, or depress-
ing; but a tenderness of conscience which dreads the
tiniest cloud on the inner sky, such as might overshadow
for a single moment the clear shining of the Father's
face. So the brief days of sojourning pass quickly on,
and the vision of the Homeland beckons to us, and bids
us mend our pace.

8

REDEEMED BY BLOOD

*"Forasmuch as ye know that ye were not redeemed
with corruptible things, as silver and gold, from your
vain conversation received by tradition from your fathers;
but with the precious blood of Christ, as of a lamb
without blemish and without spot: who, verily, was fore-
ordained before the foundation of the world, but was
manifest in these last times for you, who by Him do believe in God that raised Him up from the dead, and gave
Him glory; that your faith and hope might be in God."*
—1 PETER 1:18—21.

We belong to a redeemed race (1 Tim. 2:6). The majority
of men do not know this. Others, knowing it, do not
allow their knowledge to influence their life or conduct,
but sell their birthright for a mess of pottage. Happy are
they who not only hold the fact of redemption as an
intellectual acquisition, but permit it to become the
moulding principle of their entire life. To such the
words of the Apostle come with marvellous directness
and force. "Ye *know* that ye were redeemed."

Probably the most momentous truth about us is—that
we have been redeemed. *It is much to have been created*
—called into being by the distinct fiat of the Creator's
will. *It is much to be endowed with life* in a world so full
of marvellous possibilities as ours. *It is much to have a*

soul, which can call up the past, or interrogate the present, or anticipate the future. *But it is more that we have been redeemed.* Redeemed, as Israel from the bondage and tyranny of Egypt; or as a slave, by his "goel"—his kinsman-redeemer—from captivity to some rich creditor; or as the captive of some hideous vice emancipated from its thrall. Redeemed! Bought! Ransomed! Not that heaven is bought for us, but we bought for heaven. This will perhaps distinguish us for evermore among all other created intelligences.

I. THE COST OF OUR REDEMPTION HAS BEEN IMMENSE. (1) *Negatively.*—"Not with corruptible things, as silver and gold." A moneyed man, who has been accustomed to look on his wealth as the key to every treasure-chest, is sometimes startled to find how little it can really do. It touches the rim and circumference of life; but it fails utterly in questions that affect the heart of human existence. Money cannot compensate for broken vows; or unsay cruel words which eat into the soul like acid; or bring back colour to the pallid cheek of the darling, cold and still in death; or atone for the lack of love. "If a man would give all the substance of his house for love, it would utterly be contemned." Money can only purchase things which are as corruptible as itself; but when it enters or seeks to enter into the sphere of souls, the eternal and incorruptible, its way is barred; its currency will not pass; its claims to be heard are nonsuited.

You cannot dissect an argument with a knife, or measure love by the yard measure, or weigh souls by avoirdupois. And it is equally impossible to ransom them from sin by "corruptible things, as silver and gold." There is nothing in common between the gold and silver, which, however long they endure, must perish in the end, and the soul, which is of ethereal temper, impervious to destruction and decay, and destined to survive the crash of matter and the wreck of worlds.

God could have given suns of gold, and stars of silver, constellations glowing with precious metals; but none of these would have been sufficient to free one soul from the curse or penalty of sin, or to change it into a loyal and loving subject of his reign. Though the scales of the universe groaned on the one side with the heaped treasures of heaven, the jewels of its walls, the gold of its pavements—yet one soul placed on the other would outweigh them all. Matter accounts for nothing in the weighing-in chamber of eternity. And therefore the Creator must give not *things,* but life—not his gifts, but Himself —ere He could redeem.

(2) *Positively.*—"But with the precious blood of Christ." The blood is the life of all flesh. Life is man's supreme possession, and God's supreme gift. To give up anything less than life is to fall short of the completest self-sacrifice for another. But when a man has given that, he has given all he can. And, in addition, when blood is mentioned with the laying down of life, there is the further thought of suddenness, of intense suffering, of violence; yea, more, no one familiar with Leviticus, and with that whole system in which the Apostle Peter was educated from boyhood, could ever encounter such a reference as this without being instantly reminded of that sacrificial system, in which lambs were offered up day by day for the sins of the people.

When the Apostle speaks of being redeemed by the blood of Christ, "as of a lamb without blemish and without spot," he not only refers to the agony, and violence, and circumstances of his death, but gives renewed utterance to that first conception about the Lord which had fallen upon his ear from the lips of the great forerunner. And there can be no doubt that he desires clearly to connect the sufferer of Calvary with the lambs daily offered in the morning and evening Temple worship; with those slain at the great annual feast of the Passover; and with others, whose blood was constantly flowing to make an atonement for sin and sins.

In considering the number of lambs sacrificed in the Jewish temple, we must always remember that a large portion of their flesh was eaten, whether by the priests or the offerers; and that every method was adopted to keep the sacred structure pure, and sweet, and clean. And when we once admit that it is the office of the lower orders of creation to subserve the necessary interests of man, there is not much difference between their dying to set forth in type great spiritual truths, which are the life and soul, or to provide suitable nutriment for the sustenance of the body. But, let me repeat, in the Jewish sacrifices these two objects were most frequently combined.

It is most important to give due weight to the suggestion of this passage, which is corroborated by many similar ones throughout the Bible, that *the death of Christ was no afterthought* consequent on man's fall, but was determined before the foundation of the world. Before the mountains were brought forth, or the stars were rolled on their wondrous paths, or the first ray of light shot through the gloom, in the thought and purpose of God, our Lord was already the Lamb slain. "He was fore-ordained (designated or set apart) from before the foundation of the world" (ver. 20 ; Rev. 13 : 8).

And so the sacrifices of the Jewish ritual were in fact "the copies of things in the heavens." When Moses went up into the Mount, it is probable that he was permitted to behold the Divine purpose and plan of man's redemption ; which, as it passed before his thought, took shape in that symbolism of priest, and sacrifice, and rite, which was God's method of tuition to the chosen people, affording a rudimentary and material outline of eternal realities.

We must not think that Calvary was moulded on Leviticus, but that Leviticus was moulded on Calvary, as it stood out from all eternity before the mind of God. Yet it is unmistakable that Leviticus furnishes the true key to the understanding of the death of the cross. In those earlier books the Holy Spirit supplies us with the nomenclature and terms which He was afterwards going to employ. And just as it would be absurd to try to understand the deductions of Euclid, without first studying his definitions, so it is in vain to attempt the solution of the marvels of the cross, without entering into the force and meaning of the rites and sacrifices of the ancient Hebrew system.

Now, if there is one thing more clear than another in the Levitical sacrifices, it is the substitution of the innocent for the guilty ; and it is under this aspect that we must consider the death of our Redeemer. It is in this sense that He gave Himself for us. And this is the reason why the Apostle lays such emphasis on the *preciousness* of the sacrifice. Anything less than the costliest blood would not have availed ; because it must not be simply the blood of an individual sufferer, but of One who could suffer for a race of sinners.

The blood of Christ was precious, because of the dignity of his nature, and because of his perfect character. "Without blemish"—that is, without personal sin. "Without spot"—that is, not defiled by contact with sinners (ver. 19). Lamblike in meekness, gentleness, purity, and uncomplaining suffering. And thus it was adequate for the work of cleansing away the terrible aggregate of sin. Oh, precious blood! Oh, sacred heart of Jesus, from which it flowed, holy, loving, tender! Oh, snowy whiteness of robes washed in that fountain, and purer than the snow!

II. THE OBJECT OF OUR REDEMPTION.—"From your vain conversation received by tradition from your fathers." Do we sufficiently realise the position into which the shedding of the blood of Jesus has brought us who believe? It is our ransom price, the purchase-money of our entire being to be Christ's. The Apostles lived in the days of a merciless form of slavery; but they never hesitated to borrow from it the imagery by which to set forth our relationship to our Saviour. "Not your own, but bought with a price." "Denying the Lord who bought them" (1 Cor. 6 : 19, 20 ; 7 : 23 ; 2 Pet. 2 : 1).

The purchaser of any slave regarded him as his chattel, his goods. He could, if he chose, fling him to feed his lampreys, and none might remonstrate or punish. He looked on all his belongings, and earnings, and talents, as so much emolument for himself. His word and will were absolute law. Such are the rights which our glorious Master has over us. He has redeemed us from the curse and penalty of sin to be a people for possession—HIS VERY OWN.

Who then of us can live as we have been wont, following after vanity, treading in the footsteps of our forefathers, content to do as others before us? New claims have come in. Our Redeemer is Lord. As He has set us free from the curse and penalty of sin, so now He demands of us to come out and be separate for Himself ; leaving the husks for bread ; the bubble for the substance ; the vain conversation received by tradition, for purity, holiness, and devotion to Himself.

What a marvellous exchange there is for us in Jesus Christ! Our "vain manner of life" (R.V.) exchanged for "holiness in all manner of living" (ver. 15, R.V.) ; our imitation of our "fathers" for the upward following of Him who was raised from the dead to glory ; our reliance on "tradition" for vital contact with Christ Himself.

Have *you* assumed this attitude? If not, without delay confess with tears that you have robbed your rightful Master ; recognise his claims ; give up yourself entirely to his service ; and let the time past more than "suffice" you to have followed the tradition of the fathers with their vanities and sins. The blood of Jesus, like that of Asahel shed on the pathway of the warriors, shall make us halt in our career, and turn us on to a better mind.

III. THE CHARACTERISTIC OF THE REDEEMED.—"Who by Him do believe in God." Our faith and hope, which at the beginning of our Christian life are mainly occupied with Christ, so that we find ourselves most often addressing Him in prayer, pass through Him, who is God, to the Eternal God. The Son reveals the Father as He promised (John 14:7 9). The Father is known and loved through the Son. God becomes All in all; and the soul is satisfied to repose its entire weight on Him who has raised and glorified our Blessed Lord.

It becomes us to ponder well this important passage, attesting as it does a momentous truth. Let us not forget that the true and ultimate object of our faith must be the God of the Resurrection; the Father of our Lord; Jehovah, in whom the elders believed. And let it also be borne in mind that one primary object of the wondrous revelation of the Father in the person and work of Jesus has been to make it a little more easy for our trembling and sin-stricken souls to believe in Him. "He raised Him up and gave Him glory, that our faith and hope might be in God."

9

CHRISTIAN LOVE

"Seeing ye have purified your souls in obeying the truth through the Spirit unto unfeigned love of the brethren, see that ye love one another with a pure heart fervently: being born again, not of corruptible seed, but of incorruptible, by the Word of God, which liveth and abideth for ever."—1 PETER 1:22, 23.

We love the Lord whom we have not seen (8). We must also love our brethren whom we have seen. The latter indeed is the test of the former. "He that loveth not his brother whom he hath seen, how can he love God, whom he hath not seen?" (1 John 4:20). "See that ye love one another."

But such love is not an easy thing. We are inclined to read such an exhortation as this, and go our way, saying,

"Oh yes, this is all we need do. We must love every one, and especially those who belong to the same Christian church as ourselves—*our brethren.*" And what is the love to which we set ourselves? Is it not too often an easy sentimentality? To give things away: to indulge every wish and whim: to make things easy and pleasant all round: to wear a gracious smile—this is too often the life which we propose to ourselves, as the carrying out of the precepts of universal love. And for some temperaments this is the easiest life possible. They are naturally affable, pleasant, genial, and generous. But does this fulfil the repeated injunction of the New Testament, that we should love one another "as Christ has loved us"? For, after all, there is often a species of refined selfishness in our apparent courtesy, which desires to stand well with all, or shrinks from taking too much trouble.

What is that love of which our Lord and his Apostle speak? Not only, or primarily, kind feelings, or generous impulses. Not certainly the sentimentality which breathes itself out in sighs and raptures. Not merely the fond attachment which clings as the rose against the trellis. But, above all things, service—ministry—self-denial and self-giving. To put another's well-being before our own—not because it is pleasant to do it, but because it is right. To make another pivot around which the wheel of activity revolves. To give oneself to death a hundred times a day in unobtrusive, trifling acts of self-denial. To check the hasty word, the unkind speech, the damaging criticism. To vacate a comfortable seat in a railway carriage for the sake of the love of God. To lead a little child home, when lost in the street, or in an agony of terror from a thunderstorm, to win the "*inasmuch.*" To show to the inmates of one's home, in the most trifling incidents, the same behaviour as is prompted in men of the world by mere politeness ; and to do it for the sake of Jesus. All these things are traits of love which has no native origin in human hearts, but emanates from the being of God, descending into the hearts of his own, and passing back through them to Him again. And this is what God asks of us. Let us examine the marks of such love ; its efficient cause ; its Divine origin. And may the Holy Spirit, whose firstfruit is "love" (Gal. v. 22). shed it abroad abundantly within our hearts.

I. THE MARKS OF SUCH LOVE.

(1) *Unfeigned.*—Dissimulation is a disease very antagonistic to Christian love. More than once we are warned against it in the Apostlic writings (Rom. 12:9; 2 Cor. 6:6). We are all tempted to profess more than we feel; to kiss those whom we are betraying; to cover with soft words crevasses which are yawning deeper every day. How much more effusive we are to our friends than our thoughts of them sometimes warrant! How often we are one thing to their face and another to their back! How subtly we are tempted to maintain appearances, because of some ulterior gain!

Our politeness is often but skin-deep. Our smiles assumed for a purpose. Our words smoother than butter, whilst our hearts are drawn swords. Our acceptance of apologies, as superficial as Joseph's brethren thought that his would prove to be after old Jacob's death. Our love is not altogether "unfeigned."

(2) *Pure*—"Hearts may be cemented by impurity, by ungodly conversation and society in sin, as in uncleanness or drunkenness. The mutual love of Christians must be pure, from such causes as are pure and spiritual, arising out of the Saviour's command or example." The eye of the heart must be single; its habit stainless; its motives "white as the light." There must be no thought or suspicion of the passions of the flesh, which lie so near to the springs of intense spirituality in men and women. The love of the world so often ends in lust; lofty ideals are shattered; cloudless mornings become overcast. And our temptation lies in the same direction. It is a mistake to think that, because we meet in religious assemblies, and talk of hymns, and sermons, and sacred themes, there is no danger of the taint of impurity destroying the delicate sensitive bloom of our spirits. Too often our love is not pure.

(3) *Fervently.*—Our love seldom gets beyond "temperate," and never to boiling point. We have not learnt the secret of the heart bubbling over. We are not *fervent* in our love. We do not weep over our brethren's faults; or rejoice in their success as much as in our own; or love them with a passion which should act as an alembic for the evil that is in them.

It was the Master's last prayer that we should love like this. He meant that we should put off anger, wrath, malice, and evil speaking; and that we should put on bowels of mercies, kindness, longsuffering, and forbearance. So would the world believe (John 17: 21).

II. THE EFFICIENT CAUSE OF SUCH LOVE.—It will come through "obeying the truth." This is very marvellous. We should have thought that our love to each other would have been promoted best by meeting for social enjoyment, by knowing each other better, by constant association in Christian work. But this is not God's way. The true lens by which hearts are made to glow is the Truth.

We must know the truth.—Put two burnished mirrors opposite each other, and there will be no glow of light on either; but if a candle stand between, the beams of light are flung to and fro, to an extent impossible to either or both alone. So the mere contact of Christian with Christian will not necessarily produce the burning heart, unless there be also between them the Truth of God.

Study the lives of the saintliest men; and you will find it to have been their invariable experience, that their love to God and man grew in the precise proportion in which they explored the treasures of Divine truth. It was when their intellects were most engaged in discovering the depths of the riches both of the wisdom and knowledge of God, that their hearts seemed in a rapture of irrepressible and inexpressible ecstasy. "Did not our heart burn within us while He opened to us the Scriptures?"

We must also obey the truth.—Do, and you shall know. Obey, and you will love. Some try to promote love by the use of endearing epithets; or by the endless repetition of experience; or by reading rapturous expressions, like those which were so natural to a Bernard or a Rutherford. But such endeavours will soon wear themselves out.

A thousand times better shall we find it to set ourselves to "obey the truth." Let no command lie unfulfilled in some dusty corner of the soul. Let no margin intervene between your feet and the limit of your light. Let the life follow the Divine Word as closely as the great Lawgiver followed the cloud sailing majestically through the heavens. Translate all precepts into the vernacular of daily duty; and you will verify, in a yet deeper sense than ever, the Master's words: "He that hath my commandments and keepeth them, he it is that loveth Me" (John 14: 21).

As we obey the truth, we shall be purified by it.—Young

58

men cleanse their way by taking heed thereto according to the Divine Word. The Bridegroom purifies his bride by the washing of water through the Word. Oh, all ye who groan under the sense of a defiled heart—here is one secret of cleanliness, *Obey the truth!*

Many will read these lines who are athirst for purity and love. Innocence can never be theirs—the innocence that consists in ignorance of evil and unconsciousness of temptation. But they desire that purity which passes through evil untainted, as sunbeams through a fœtid atmosphere, and for that love which floods cannot drown, like the old Greek fire which burnt under water.

The atheist does not think that these things are possible. He has no hope in God, and no belief in man. He looks darkly on all profession, and sadly suspects every motive. Oh, do not let your high hopes be dashed or your ambitions lowered by his suggestions. Undaunted, still seek for the holy grail of a pure and burning heart, It shall certainly reward your search at last.

There is no need to seek this blessed gift in the wilderness, like St. Anthony; on the pillar, like Simon Stylites; in the recesses of the forest, like Gaudama. "The word is nigh thee, in thy mouth and in thy heart" (Rom. 10: 8). *Purify your heart in obeying the truth unto unfeigned love of the brethren.*

Nor will it be difficult to understand how it is that so simple a method will achieve so great a result, when we have given the next consideration its true weight.

III. THE DIVINE ORIGIN OF THE LIFE WITHIN.— "Having been begotten again" (23, R.V.). Our spiritual life is "not of the will of the flesh, nor of the will of man, but of God" (John 1:13). We have been twice born. Born once by nature into the stock of the first Adam; and born a second time by grace into the stock of the second Adam, the Lord from heaven. "Of his own will God begat us by the word of truth, that we should be a kind of first-fruits of his creatures" (James 1:18). One chief evidence of this life is simple trust in the Saviour. As many as believe in his name were born (John 1:13).

And the life that has been implanted within us is like the inheritance which awaits us (4) and the blood which purchased us (18)—INCORRUPTIBLE. It cannot, therefore, be limited by the narrow landmarks of time, or sense, or this fleeting world. It overleaps and defies them all. It partakes of the nature of the Infinite and Eternal. Thus it follows that the piety it effects is of celestial temper, and the love it manifests is the true unfeigned love of Deity. The best guarantee of the permanence and reality of Christian Purity and Love is to look at the life from which they emanate, and which is implanted by the second birth—a life which in turn is best considered in the seed from which it has come, and by which it has been communicated to the believer's heart.

That seed is here contrasted with the outward life of men. *All flesh is as grass:* men and women pass away as the successive crops on the meadows. *And the glory of man as the flower of grass.* The king-cups and daisies share the fate of the lowely blades around them, emblems of the impotence of wealth or strength or beauty to resist the ravages of the sickle of Time. But in contrast to this stands out the eternal Truth of God, which is enshrined in the holy words of God. It is LIVING and lifegiving. It remaineth and "abideth for ever."

That the Bible is amongst us to-day—in spite of all that has been done to destroy it, by fire, and search, and sword—attests the fact that there are properties in it which divide it by an impassable chasm from all books beside. It is clearly true of all Scripture words, that they "are spirit and life," and can never pass away; and that not one jot or tittle shall fail. And this fact that the Bible lives and abides, notwithstanding all that has been done against it, proves that it possesses something of the life of the eternal and infinite God. God is manifestly in this Book, as of old in the acacia bush of the desert; or as natural life burns like a tiny spark within each seed falling down the bank. The persistence of the Book proves God to be in it. And therefore it is God's life which enters dead human souls through the Word and makes them live. The life which is thus begotten in them is infinite and eternal as Himself. And, being so, it lifts its possessors above the time-sphere into the very realm of heaven, and enables them to love, not with the poor faltering love of man, but with the royal, pure, unfeigned, blessed love, which is the very soul of the life of God Himself.

10

GOD'S NEW-BORN BABES AND THEIR FOOD

"Wherefore laying aside all malice, and all guile, and hypocrisies, and envies, and all evil speakings, as newborn babes, desire the sincere milk of the Word, that ye may grow thereby; if so be ye have tasted that the Lord is gracious."—1 PETER 2: 1—3.

This paragraph is closely connected with the preceding one. In that we learnt how we had been born again, and entered by the new birth into the family of God. Here the same thought is resumed. We are addressed as the babes of the Divine family, and bidden to cultivate the temper and seek the nourishment suitable to a relationship at once so blessed and hallowed.

I. OUR CONDITION AS GOD'S LITTLE ONES.—"New-born babes." The metaphor is a very touching one. This world is but the nursery in which the heirs of God are spending the first lisping years of their existence, preparatory to the opening of life to full maturity yonder in the light of God. The most advanced among us, in knowledge and attainment, are, in comparison with what they shall be, only as babes. The furthest stretch of vision, the most perfect conceptions of the intellect, the fittest expressions of truth, are but as the untutored thoughts and babblings of babyhood, compared with what is to be in the mature life which beckons us yonder.

The same idea is expressed by the Apostle Paul in his exquisite idyll on Christian love. He is endeavouring to show that this fairest of the whole band of Christian graces is eternal in its nature, budding here, defying the frosts of death, and blooming in heaven's everlasting summer. And, to make his conception more emphatic, he contrasts love with knowledge, affirming that our profoundest knowledge must vanish away, because in this life we are but children. "When I was a child I spake as a child, I understood as a child, I thought as a child; but when I became a man, I put away childish things." And, similarly, in the next life, while we retain the love which we have had in this, we shall put away the knowledge as partial and immature, because from being children we shall have become men in Christ. We need not concern ourselves now with all the majestic conceptions which cluster around those words: it is enough to notice the thought, that the Apostle Paul considered himself a little child, compared with the coming maturity of eternity.

This word should teach us *Humility*. "Our best pace and strongest walking in obedience here is but as the stepping of children when they begin to go by hold, in comparison with the perfect obedience of glory, when we shall follow the Lamb whithersoever He goeth. All our knowledge here is but as the ignorance of infants, and all our expressions of God and of his praises but as the first stammerings of children, in comparison with the knowledge we shall have of Him hereafter, when we shall know as we are known, and with the praises we shall offer to Him, when that 'new song' shall be taught us." It becomes us, therefore, not to exercise ourselves in great matters, or in things too high for us, but to quiet ourselves as a child that is weaned of its mother, so that our souls may be even as a weaned child. Not surprised, if unnoticed or unknown; not angry, if treated with small respect; not discouraged, if face to face with incomprehensible mysteries. Our intellect is only in its dawn, our powers undeveloped, our mental grasp limited. Far be from us the haughty heart, the proud look, the conceited opinion, the sweeping assertion of self-satisfaction. Ours is the lisp of infancy: "Abba."

This word should also teach us *Hope*. There is no young thing so helpless as a babe, or for so long dependent on its parents' care. But He who has appointed the long months of babyhood has also provided the love and patience with which mother and father welcome and tend the strange wee thing which has come into their home. It is not often that a woman can forget her sucking child, that she should not have compassion on her son. Through ailments and sickness, days of anxiety, and nights of watching; with love which never considers cost, or pain, or self-denial—two fond guardian angels care for the babe. Its least cry will compel the service of a man dreaded by all his comrades, and noted for the strength and independence of his character. And shall God have put into others qualities in which He is

Himself deficient? Shall He have provided so carefully for us in our first birth, and have provided nought in our second? Is not the very love of the human parent a parable of that of the Divine? Is He not Mother and Father both?

It must be so. Since He has begotten us into his family, He must have to us the love of a parent to a babe; and we must have a claim on Him, as the babe on its parent. The more utterly helpless, and ignorant, and dependent the babe is, the stronger is its claim. Yes, and the more puny and sickly it is, the more urgent are its demands for tender solicitude and attention, till the spark of life, shaded by loving hands from the least unkindly breath, grows strong within the tiny lantern. Who is angry with a child because it is weakly, sick, and dull of brain? Who does not find in these things the reason for greater tenderness, so that mothers are said to love most the children who have cost them most? And is it not so with God? Your weakness, and ailments, and nervous dread, and besetting sins, and hereditary taint of evil habit, and dullness of vision, will not drive God from you, but will bring Him nearer. These things will draw down his choicest love to your poor-cradled being. He will sit beside you as a nurse. He will watch your every change. He will care for you with unslumbering thoughtfulness. He will supply your every need. He will make you know things hidden from the wise and prudent, but revealed to babes, in words which even they can understand. He will never leave you until you are reared to the perfect beauty of maturity in Christ.

This word should also teach us our true *attitude towards God*. Throw yourself on Him with the abandonment of a babe. Roll on Him the responsibility of choosing for you—directing, protecting, and delivering you. If you cannot understand his will, expect Him to make it plain. If you cannot feel as you would, believe that his feeling towards you is unalterable as a father's. If you are overcome by sin, be sure that it cannot alienate his love, any more than can the small-pox, which has marred some dear tiny face, prevent the mother from kissing the little parched lips. Oh, strong men and women, never get so strong as to cease to remember that you are the babes of God, and that you may carry out this winsome similitude to the full! Listen to his declaration: "I have nourished and brought up children."

II. OUR FOOD.—"Long for the spiritual milk which is without guile" (R.V.) At the close of the previous chapter the Word of God was compared with seed; here, with milk. But it is the same principle under different aspects. The new life is nourished by that through which it was first imparted. There are deep analogies between the worlds of nature and of grace, attesting the unity of design which pervades the universe, making the seen and the unseen one great whole.

There is nothing which so proves the inspiration of the Scriptures as their suitableness to the nurture of the new life in the soul. As long as that life is absent, there is no special charm in the sacred Word: it lies unnoticed on the shelf. But directly the new life has been implanted, and whilst yet in its earliest stages, it seeks after the Word of God as a babe after its mother's milk; and instantly it begins to grow. This affinity between the Divine life in the soul and the sacred Scriptures establishes their emanation from the same source as gave it birth. Human life in infancy is most naturally nourished by the products of the life from which it originated; and since the Divine life in man is nourished by the words of the Bible, surely *it* also is proved to be Divine in its origin, supernatural in its qualities, heavenly in its temper—as far removed from the earthly and human as is the life to which it ministers.

Oh, well would it be if we were to minister to the regenerated spirits around us more of the pure and unadulterated Word of God! It is this which they really need. They may be attracted and pleased for a time by flowers of rhetoric and the dazzling glow of eloquence; but they will not be *satisfied* by these things. Underneath all there will be a greater hunger for the sincere milk of the Word. And when that word is presented in all its fullness and simplicity, eager appetites will gather around as bees attracted by the flower-gardens, or the fragrant growth of the heather. "Before conversion, wit or eloquence may draw a man to the Word, and possibly prove a happy bait to catch him; but when once he is born again then it is the milk itself that he desires."

And here surely we are taught the reason why so many Christians around us are so puny and stunted in their growth. They are always needing attention, nursing, wheeling about in perambulators, because their teachers have not provided them with the nutriment which they really need. An unsuitable food, however abundant, will soon tell its own tale on the pinched face of a babe, so the sickly condition of so many Christians sets forth a lamentable complaint of the food with which they are supplied. To say nothing of strong meat, they do not even get milk. Hence the Church of God too much resembles the wards of a children's hospital.

III. HOW TO CREATE AN APPETITE FOR THE WORD.—"Desire." One of the most dangerous symptoms is the loss of appetite. It is the danger-signal warning that evil lurks unseen within. And there is no surer indication of religious declension and ill-health than the cessation of desire for the Word of God. How can that appetite be created where lacking, and stimulated where declining? The answer is given in the context.

(1) *Put off the evil that clings to you.*—The word translated "putting away" is the same as in Col. 3:8. The idea is the change of dress which is often used as a Scriptural figure for the change of the habit of the soul. The habiliments which we must doff are enumerated, and a terrible catalogue it is. Alas that it should ever have been necessary, or that it should still be, to urge Christians to surrender such obvious evils as these!

Malice, which is anger cooled down into "double-distilled malignity," rejoicing in the misfortunes which come to others. *Guile,* which savours of trick and craft. *Hypocrisy,* the Judas-act of concealing treachery beneath the garb of friendship. *Envy,* which repines at another's good. Both malice and envy vent themselves in *evil speaking.* These things spoil the appetite for God's Word, as surely as sweetmeats clog the physical appetite and taste. Many cannot enjoy the Word of God, because their minds are so occupied with these poisoned dainties, or with the sugar-coated sweetmeats of exciting or questionable literature, of worldy amusements, and of evil imaginings. These things must be at once and for ever put away. You must elect the cross. There must be a casting aside of the shameful works of darkness, so only can the appetite for God's Word become vigorous and eager. Clear away the rubbish, and the spring will burst up naturally from the ground.

(2) *Remember that your growth depends on your feeding on the Word.*—Who is there amongst us that is not anxious to grow; to become more Christlike, and holy, and devoted; to increase in knowledge and in grace? But we appear often to imagine that we shall grow by

attending meetings or doing Christian work. It is a disastrous mistake. And until we come to see that growth is proportionate to Bible-study, it will be impossible to rise up to the perfect beauty of the stature of Christ. We shall always be children, carried about by every wind of doctrine.

Do not always read your Bible because you like to do so, or desire it, but because it is right to do it, and as a matter of simple duty to your own life. Study the Word under the light of the Holy Spirit, as the ancient saint, when blindness was setting in, was wont to carry his Bible to the window, and place the open page in the full beams of the western sun. And slowly the appetite will re-assert itself, and you will come to esteem the Word of God more than your necessary food.

(3) *Stimulate your desire by the memory of past enjoyment.*—"If so be that ye have tasted that the Lord is gracious." We seek food, not only because our body requires it, but because we remember the past sweetness of it to our taste. We often take more than is necessary to appease hunger, because the food is toothsome.

How sweet to the taste is the precious Lord! For none among the sons and daughters of men can be compared to Him. His love has sometimes filled our souls with inexpressible delight and bliss—grapes of Eschol, prelibations of the river of life, branches laden with fruit reaching over the wall. And those who have once tasted of that love have contracted a passion which grows in being fed. Because they have tasted they must come again and again to stay an appetite which, though always being met, is always on the increase.

Do you not remember days like these, of feasting and song, when you were led into his banqueting-house, or sat under his shadow with great delight? If so, surely the memory of them will sharpen the jaded desire, until it cries with the spouse: "Stay me with flagons, comfort me with apples; for I am sick of love." Ah, how vapid and insipid do the joys of the world appear when once the soul has tasted that the Lord is gracious. "Taste and see that the Lord is good: blessed is the man that trusteth in Him."

11

THE PRECIOUS CORNER-STONE

"To whom coming, as unto a living stone, disallowed indeed of men, but chosen of God, and precious, ye also as lively stones are built up a spiritual house, an holy priesthood, to offer up spiritual sacrifices acceptable to God by Jesus Christ. Wherefore also it is contained in the Scripture, Behold, I lay in Sion a chief corner-stone, elect, precious: and he that believeth on Him shall not be confounded. Unto you therefore which believe He is precious: but unto them which be disobedient, the stone which the builders disallowed, the same is made the head of the corner, and a stone of stumbling, and a rock of offence, even to them which stumble at the Word, being disobedient: whereunto also they were appointed. But ye are a chosen generation, a royal priesthood, an holy nation, a peculiar people: that ye should show forth the praises of Him who hath called you out of darkness into his marvellous light: which in time past were not a people, but are now the people of God; which had not obtained mercy, but now have obtained mercy."—1 PETER 2: 4-10.

Peter, "surnamed Cephas, which is by interpretation a stone," has much to say about his Master as the stone; and weaves together into a beautiful mosaic the many allusions which convey this aspect of his character and work, sparkling as jewels on the page of Scripture.

In the hieroglyphed chamber in Egypt, where Jacob lay a-dying, his mind reverted to the massive stones which were strewn over his native land, and which on one occasion had figured so strangely in his dreams; and he spake of the coming Shepherd as being the "Stone of Israel." Moses in his swan-song, when bidding the people ascribe greatness to God, alleged as the reason, "He is the Rock." And David, in the last of his Psalms, opened his exquisite delineation of the true King by saying, "The Rock of Israel spake to me."

New interest was given to the same thought by an incident which is said to have occurred in the building of Solomon's Temple. The stones were shaped at a distance from the sacred site, that no sound of chisel or stone-saw might be heard during the building of that house for God.

As the palm of the desert, or the oak of the forest, grows noiselessly into perfect maturity and beauty, so did that noble pile crown the summit of Zion. But on one occasion a stone was brought up by the straining oxen, which refused to fit into any of the rising walls. And, after repeated attempts to dispose of it, it was placed by itself in a retired spot, and was soon forgotten, perhaps even covered by a luxuriant growth of weeds. At last, as the building neared completion, it was discovered that a stone of special form would be required to knit two walls, and fill a particular corner. The need suggested the forgotten and rejected bit of masonry, which was lying still where it had been discarded. "The stone which the builders refused became the head-stone of the corner." This incident is said to have suggested that reference of the venerable Psalm, which is quoted by the Lord as applying to Himself, and is referred to in at least two other places in the New Testament besides this (Psa. 118: 22 ; Matt. 21: 42 ; Mark 12: 10 ; Luke 20: 17 ; Acts 4: 11 ; Eph. 2: 20).

In a slightly different form, the same thought re-appears in Isaiah. The men of his time were full of the project of a foreign alliance as the best means of bolstering up the kingdom, just then in dire peril of dissolution, through internal dissension and threatening invasion. God, by the mouth of his prophet, compared the attempt, and the peace it gave, to making a covenant with death, and a hiding-place of lies, and foretold the breaking of a storm, in which none of these devices should avail to shield their inventors. And then, in answer to the dread with which his own people foreboded the fury of that hail, and the overflowing of those waters, He said that He would lay in Zion, for a foundation, "a stone—a tried stone—a precious corner stone, a sure foundation" ; and that He who belived should not make haste.

Daniel adds one further link to the chain of holy thought, when he likens the kingdom of God to the quarrying of a mighty stone in some lone mountain rent. Though no hands are engaged upon it, it assumes shape, disintegrates itself from its rocky home, and begins to roll down the mountain side crushing everything obstructing its path. If that stone is for a moment still, and a man falls over it, he is broken and maimed. It is "a stone of stumbling, and a rock of offence." If, on the other hand, it falls on some passer-by it grinds him to powder. In many a highland valley, standing out amid the green grass, on which the sheep peacefully browse in summer, there are mighty masses of rock which have leapt from the face of the overhanging cliffs. Woe to any man who had been standing beneath at the moment of their fall! Battered—demolished—ground to powder. These are solemn words. But they are adapted from the prophecies of Daniel by the Master himself (Dan. 2:34; Matt. 21:44).

I. LET US TRY TO UNDERSTAND THE CONCEPTION OF THE PARAGRAPH.—It is full of changing metaphor; image piled on image; thought sliding into thought, and rising in noble sequence to a pitch of sublime magnificence. On a massive bed of Rock, there lies a *Stone,* which is fitted to be a bond of union, joining lines of building, which had run in opposite directions, making "both one." It is not only a stone, it is a *corner stone* (Eph. 2:20).

Behold that stone! God looks on it with his sevenfold omniscience; and his hands have engraved on it rare symbols of mystery and beauty, such as no skilled human hand could design (Zech. 3:9). The carved lily work of Jachin and Boaz even could not vie with that heavenly workmanship. How manifestly is this stone both *elect* and *precious*. Jesus was *elect* before all worlds, as the organ of creation, the channel of redemption, the head of the new race, the foundation-stone of the Church. And as to his dignity and worth, He is *beyond all price,* the pearl of inestimable value, the Koh-i-noor of heaven, the fairest among ten thousand, the altogether lovely, the jewel of God's heart.

Next: there might be imagined an altercation among the builders. Though the stone lies there ready to their hand, they deliberately reject God's prepared foundation. Some are inclined to admire the carving, or to praise the situation selected for it. But more criticise it, or deride it, or account it as only suitable to carry part of their scaffolding. And so after some discussion, the builders, wise in their own judgment, pass away. "Disallowed indeed of men"! And then, without foundations, they begin an erection, which is built on a seam of sand,

and is destined to stand as an unfinished monument of their folly.

But God's purpose cannot be foiled. If men will not build on his foundation, yet there shall still stand on it a structure to his eternal praise. Here is a marvel indeed! For, lo! the stone *lives*. "A living stone." "It is full of eyes." Nay, more, it is attractive as magnetised iron: it draws to itself other stones, dead, heavy, hard, which are lying all around; and as one after another they slowly approach it, they also begin to live. "To whom coming, a living stone, ye also, as *living stones*." But even here the marvel does not stay. As in the prophet's vision, bone after bone disentangled itself from the heaps of the slain, and built itself up into the order and symmetry of the human frame, so here stone follows stone, as if gathered by unseen hands, and together they build up a house, the fabric of which is not material, but spiritual; because, as the stones have passed into life, they have dropped their grosser nature, and have become etherealised into a spirituality of essence, befitting the constituent parts of "a spiritual house." God, whose home is in "the high and holy place," dwells also in the "house" composed of saved and saintly spirits, once gross, material, dead as stones, but now, by contact with Jesus Christ, made pure, holy, and, in the deepest sense, *spiritually-minded*. "This is my rest for ever: here will I dwell; for I have desired it."

But in such a temple there must be priests; and in this also the Divine purpose cannot fail. Those who were once but as the rubble of the hillside, are not only constituted part of a spiritual fabric, but by a rapid change in the thought, they are represented as performing priestly functions, *an holy priesthood,* clad in the appointed garments for holiness and beauty. And since a priesthood must have somewhat to offer, and these occupants of the true temple cannot appear before the altar or tread the inner shrine, with empty hands, *there are sacrifices prepared*: yet (and the thought changes once more) these sacrifices are not material any more than they need to be propitiatory, since the one all-sufficient sacrifice for sin has been offered once for all; but they are spiritual, and consist in the consecrated lives and jubilant praises of those who have been raised from the dust *to offer up spiritual sacrifices, acceptable to God, by Jesus Christ.*

Nor is that all: those who are thus associated with

Christ are identified with Him in the esteem and love of God. In the one verse, we are told that our Lord is *precious* in the esteem of the Father—his beloved; his darling; his only one. But in the original Greek of a following verse, correctly rendered in the R.V., this preciousness is assigned to us; *for you therefore which believe is the preciousness*. Not only is Jesus precious to us, as our beloved and our friend, but his worth and beauty in the mind of God are passed on to us who believe; so that our dull common natures flash in the excellence of his loveliness. Yes, and we are changed into his likeness from glory to glory. Thus the fishermen of Galilee are discovered in the lowest tier of the foundations of the New Jerusalem, as precious stones. And what is true of them is in a measure true of us all. Iron touches magnetised iron and becomes magnetic. Stones touch *the* Stone and become jewels. Thus God manufactures his stores of precious stones, the facets of which, cut here in pain, shall flash for ever in the light of his own glory yonder.

And now, ere we turn away, let us look once more at the disobedient and disbelieving builders. Some of them have stumbled over the Divine preparation, and are hopelessly maimed; others wander out on to the dark mountains, where they will meet with many a disaster, falling down precipices, or being otherwise overtaken with death. And their proud building shall stand as a second Babel, for the laughter of the world. They are "confounded" indeed: a fate which is impossible for those who build on God's elect foundation. Alas that men should abuse the very means which God had prepared for their salvation and blessedness!

II. THE PERSONAL APPLICATION *Ye are an elect race* (R.V.).—There are elect races in the world, standing in the sunlit circle of civilisation, not for themselves only, but for others. The larger the privilege, the greater the responsibility. This is the Divine method of government through the selection of nations or races, which are specially gifted and endowed, that they may be better qualified to help and save their fellows. And the position of the Israelite nation, to whom pertained "the adoption, and the glory, and the covenants," was expressly entrusted to them, that through them God might bless all the nations of the earth. But during the present period of rejection the Christian Church has been summoned to this glorious work of becoming the channel for the Divine blessing to mankind.

A royal priesthood.—These two offices were jealously kept apart in Israel, and when Uzziah attempted to combine them he was driven from the Temple with the brand of leprosy on his brow. But in Christ they blend. "He is a priest upon his throne" (Zech. 6:13). And all his followers are constituted kings and priests (Rev. 1:6). As priests we worship in near proximity to God; as kings we rule over men with a rule born of love, which blesses and saves.

An holy nation.—This expression, like the former, comes from the ancient covenant into which God entered with Israel at Sinai (Exod. 19:6). Israel failed in keeping it, and, as a nation, they have been temporarily cast aside; but the individuals, whether Jews or Greeks, who have accepted Christ, constitute in their hosts another nation, which, as an innumerable multitude, lives throughout the world, obeying a higher morality, citizens of the city which can never pass away.

A people for God's own possession.—Love yearns for proprietorship; nor can the heart of God be satisfied unless it can speak of some as its own. Oh, happy they who have obeyed his summons, and have made a complete surrender of themselves to Him! He has already taken them for his own possession. Enclosed as a garden; tilled as a field; inhabited as a home; guarded, kept, used, loved, with an emphasis none others know. Nor is there anything in God Himself which is not at the disposal of those who hold nothing back from Him.

How can we repay Him for all that He has done for us—when we compare what we are, with what we were? Once in darkness, now in marvellous light. Once not included among the people of God, now accounted as part of them. Once without hope of mercy, now the happy recipients of untold mercy. What shall we say? Is it not our duty to praise Him, not only with our lips, but in our lives, casting our crowns at his feet, and bearing our part in the song of adoration, which from all creation breaks around his throne. Let us show forth his praise!

12

THE PLEA FOR A BLAMELESS LIFE

"Dearly beloved, I beseech you as strangers and pilgrims, abstain from fleshly lusts, which war against the soul; having your conversation honest among the Gentiles: that whereas they speak against you as evildoers, they may by your good works, which they shall behold, glorify God in the day of visitation."—1 PETER 2:11, 12.

We now pass from the more purely doctrinal to the practical. All the Apostles begin their Epistles by laying adamant foundations of Gospel truth, on which they erect a superstructure of exhortations to practical Godliness. Perhaps this division is less noticeable in the writings of the Apostle Peter than in those of his "beloved brother Paul." Still there is clearly a transition at this point. The sermon that has no personal application is a failure. Doctrine without precept tends to dry speculation. Precept without doctrine tends to a sapless formalism, destitute of power.

How tenderly these exhortations are expressed! It is not easy to realise that Peter, the strong rock-man, is speaking here. But years of sorrow have done their work, in mellowing and toning the roughness of his character. And there is a gentleness in his voice, as he beseeches his *dearly beloved* readers, which must have been one of the strongest persuasives to the life for which he pleaded. This plea for a blameless life must have gone home with double effect, because the shaft was winged with feathers drawn from love's gentle breast. The force of the expression is the greater, because it is not often that we find Peter pleading thus. Christian love does not always require the use of tender and effusive expressions. There is always a danger of their losing their meaning and power through incessant repetition; but there are occasions, especially when we yearn for the welfare of others, at which, though we might be bold enough to enjoin them that which is convenient, yet, for love's sake, we rather beseech them.

Fleshly lusts are enumerated in detail in several passages of the Word of God (Gal. 5:19 21). *Lust* is inordinate desire—the desire for too much of a good thing, or for any of a bad one. *Fleshly* lusts are those which seek their gratification through the avenues of the physical nature with which God has endowed us. We are all provided with certain natural instincts and desires, which have been implanted for right and useful purposes, and are innocent and right when regulated by the will of God. But these natural appetites are constantly fretting against restraint, yearning for unlawful gratification, seething and foaming as the sea-waves against harbour bar. If you yield to them ; if you love anything outside the circle of God's will ; if you follow your own wild instincts, irrespective of the self-restraint demanded by conscience ; if you indulge any one side of your nature out of the due balance and equilibrium of the whole ; if you allow an undue monopoly of taste or thought in one direction —then beware! You need especially to be on your guard against the fleshly lusts of which the Apostle speaks.

They war against the soul.—That word "war" is full of meaning. It gives the idea of the march of an army against a city, as of the Greeks to surround and capture Troy—an assault which began with open war and ended by the stratagem of the wooden horse, from which the armed warriors descended into the heart of the city at dead of night. Of course we should all admit that excessive indulgence in any appetite injures the body, and especially the organs through which the sin against the whole fabric has been committed. But we may not all realise how destructive these fleshly lusts are to the inner life. They attack and conquer it, and lead it into captivity, impairing its energies, sullying its purity, lowering its tone, and cutting off the locks of moral strength. Remember then, when tempted to yield to some unholy prompting, even though you only indulge the thought or wish, that you are exposing yourself to a certain diminution of spiritual force, which will inevitably cripple your endeavours, and show itself in failure and defeat. No act of sensual indulgence is possible without inevitable injury to our true selves, it may be forgiven, and put away, through the forgiveness of God, by the blood of Jesus ; but the soul can never be quite what it would have been had the temptation been overcome, and the grace of self-restraint exercised.

How many there are around us, eminently fitted by their gifts, to lead the hosts of God, who, like Samson, grind in the prison-house, making pastime for their foes, because they have been mastered by appetites which they should have controlled, as the horseman his fiery steed! Is there not a deep spiritual truth in the notion of the savage warrior, that the strength of a fallen foe enters the arm which has smitten him to the dust? Indulge the flesh—and you are weak. Curb it by self-restraint—and you are strong.

We need, however, to notice *how this abstinence from unholy indulgence may be realised*. And it may be helpful to remember the following points:—

(1) *Let us understand that self-restraint is possible.*— It is quite true that we are children of a sinning race, and come into life with the taint of evil in us. This is not a matter for argument, but of each man's individual experience. Though the third chapter of *Genesis* and the first chapter of *Romans* had never been penned, we must have felt that somewhere there had been an awful lapse in the story of our race, or that it had been the sport of some malign fate. From the first there is in us all an hereditary tendency to gratify to excess the promptings of the natural appetite. Besides this we have deepened and intensified these inherited tendencies by our actual transgressions. There have been repeated yieldings, each one of which has nourished and fostered their strength. And we resemble an athlete, who has permitted himself to be bound around with threads of cotton, any of which could be snapt in a moment, but all of which together hold him like an iron chain.

But, notwithstanding this, it is true that no temptation can happen to us but such as is common to man—none with which God cannot deal. It would be impious to say that God has permitted evil to arrive at such a pitch that He cannot cope with it; or that there is any sin, usurping his throne in the inner realm, which He cannot quell.

It is immaterial how strong may be your inherited tendencies towards evil, or the habits which you have formed by successive acts of sin—God is able to give you deliverance, and to keep you from being overcome. It is possible even for *you* to abstain from the fleshy lusts which have been subjugating your soul, as Moabites and Philistines did the fair land of Israel in the days when the Judges ruled. Every command carries a promise at its heart; and this loving entreaty for a better, purer life hides a Divine undertaking that you shall yet be more than conqueror, putting your foot on flesh and self, and reigning where now you groan in slavery. Take heart! it is possible even for *you* to abstain from fleshy lusts, because God is able to keep.

(2) *Choose death.*—There is a sense in which we all died in Jesus Christ our Lord, when on the cross He yielded up his spirit to his Father. There is also another sense in which we must die daily, in the constant denial of self. But, besides this, there must be one definite moment in each Christian's life when death is definitely chosen for all that is selfish, worldly, fleshly, and of the devil. This is surely the meaning of the Apostle, when he says, using a tense which signifies a definite past act: "They that are of Christ Jesus *crucified* the flesh with the passions and the lusts thereof" (Gal. 5:24 R.V.).

Too many of us never come to that point. We accept the incursions and reign of evil things too much as an inevitable experience to which we must ever be liable in this world. We yield, and repent, and curse ourselves, and yield again. Christians often speak of their besetting sins as natural infirmities which they cannot help, but which must be borne as the diseases incident to childhood. There is too little of the rising up of a holy and almost fierce determination to be free.

Or if there be such a resolve, it often lacks completeness. It shuts the front door but not the back door of the nature, against the thought of possible indulgence. It leaves an almost invisible thread of communication between the soul and the evils of which it would fain be rid, and along it the contagion is still free to pass. And as long as there is the smallest flaw in the integrity of the soul's purpose, there is no hope of deliverance. We must cut all connection, close every aperture, and abandon all thought of fleshly indulgence in every shape and form. In short, we must choose death.

Is not this the secret of your repeated failure? You have heard about the keeping power of Christ, and have appealed for it. But you have not been kept. You have been overcome in spite of your cries for help. And you will never get right until you go down into the grave where Jesus lay, and place yourself on that rough rocky niche, whilst the heavy stone shuts you away from all that you held dear. And when you count all things dross for his sake, you will win Christ. Through the grave you will come to the Easter dawn. Death will be the gate of life. Having been crucified with Christ, you will discover that his life will flow into you triumphantly.

With much earnestness do the pages of the New Testament appeal to us to come to this definite resolution. But especially is it the keynote of that marvellous *sixth chapter of Romans,* which appeals to us as having died with Christ, and as therefore being free from sin. Expressions are employed, from which we would have shrunk, as being too forcible, too extreme, in order to show how complete the deliverance is for those who have been with Christ in the likeness of his death. There is not the least doubt that our deliverance from the power of all fleshly lusts is in the precise measure in which we have embraced that idea of complete severance from them, which is suggested in the one final, all-severing, awful word—*Death.*

(3) *Walk in the Spirit.*—There are Christians who live in the Spirit, but who do not walk in the Spirit (Gal. 5: 25). The distinction is an obvious one. We live in the Spirit, because only in Him we share at all in the life of Christ, a life which is everlasting and Divine. But how few of us walk in the Spirit from hour to hour; pausing at each step, so that He may work or speak; looking to Him for guidance at each turn of the path; and adopting the track which He indicates, as by the cloud in old time, while moving over the desert sands!

But nothing less than this will suffice. "Walk in the Spirit," says the Apostle, "and ye shall not fulfil the lusts of the flesh." It is not enough to resolve to abstain: the mere resolution will not be sufficient to keep the door shut against the pressure of temptation. We must have something positive. Not the water of a negation, but the fire of a possession. The indwelling and pre-occupation of the Holy Spirit in his fullness can alone suffice for our need. And this can only be had by a reverent and perpetual communication being maintained between the soul and Him; as air must be pumped into the diver's helmet at every movement he makes on the ocean floor.

But when the soul is pervaded perpetually by the presence and power of the Holy Spirit, it is easy to abstain. The soul loses its very taste for things in which it formerly delighted. It detects them when yet far distant, and shudders at their approach. Satisfied with the provision of the Father's house, it turns with disgust from the husks of the swine-trough.

The motives for this abstinence are more than sufficient. (1) *We are strangers and pilgrims.*—"Consider what you are. If you were citizens of this world, then you might drive the same trade with them, and follow the same lusts; but seeing you are chosen and called out of this world, and invested into a new society, made free of another country, it is very reasonable that there be this difference betwixt you and the world, that while they live as at home, your behaviour be such as becomes strangers; not glutting yourselves with their pleasures, not surfeiting upon their delicious fruits, but living warily and soberly."

However gay or comfortable the hostelry may be, the traveller hastens homewards. It is not for him to entangle himself with the fascinations and allurements of the towns through which he goes. Indeed, he has no time to be allured; before the meshes of the net enwrap him he is gone. And the attractions of the beloved circle which await him so engage and monopolise his heart that he has no desire for the unholy baits which are offered to him. What then have we in common with fleshly lusts, when our citizenship is in heaven, whence we are looking for the Saviour?

(2) *We must consider our influence on the world.*—Our behaviour among the Gentiles must be *honest, i.e.,* fair or beautiful, not only for our sake, but for theirs. Followers of Jesus must never be surprised to find themselves spoken of as evil doers. They called the Master "Beelzebub"; how much more will they malign the slaves of Christ's household! The most monstrous stories were circulated throughout the Roman Empire of the rites which Christians were said to perpetrate in their secret meetings; and on the ground of those stories they were punished with torture and death.

Such baseless charges are sometimes made still, and we must take care not to give any occasion for them in our behaviour. Nay, we must so live, that, in the day of crisis and trial, men may be compelled to acknowledge the worth of our religion, and to glorify God for having enabled us so to bear and suffer and endure.

There are arguments being built up in sick-chambers, and in the furnaces of trial through which Christians are called to pass, which silence detractors, and compel them to admit the presence of a strength, a patience, and a fortitude, for which their philosophy cannot account. And in many such cases has blasphemy been turned to adoration, and railing to praise.

With such motives to animate us, let us give a favourable response to this touching and earnest plea for a stainless and blameless life.

13

GOD'S SLAVES

"Submit yourselves to every ordinance of man for the Lord's sake: whether it be to the king, as supreme; or unto governors, as unto them that are sent by Him for the punishment of evildoers, and for the praise of them that do well. For so is the will of God, that with well-doing ye may put to silence the ignorance of foolish men: as free, and not using your liberty for a cloke of maliciousness, but as the servants of God."—1 PETER 2:13—16.

It is very remarkable to notice the frequency and earnestness with which the writers of the New Testament insist on the use of that word "slave," as describing their true relationship to God. It is the favourite designation of the Apostle Paul, "apostle and slave," and he even gloried in wearing the brandmarks of the slavery of Jesus. Not only here, but in the first line of his Second Epistle, the Apostle Peter describes himself in the very same terms. And the Apocalyptic vision of the Apostle John rings with the word, touched with heavenly light, transfigured, glorified. That wondrous book is prepared for slaves; they are the sealed; they receive the rewards; they see God's face and bear his name upon their brows. Heaven takes our most dreaded terms, and makes them sparkle in its own light, till what had seemed the synonym of terror becomes the target of our noblest aims, The servants of the royal household are nobles.

All this is very singular. For the slavery which throve in the poisoned atmosphere of the pagan world was the most cruel and wicked thing that society has ever seen.

The slavery of the Roman Empire was slavery at its worst. The slave was the absolute chattel of his owner, for purposes of crushing labour, bitter torture, degrading crime. There was no appeal, no hope of redress, no escape, except by the dread door of death. And yet it is this system which the sacred writers never weary of applying to our relationship to Jesus Christ. It presents them with an ideal which stirs their intensest enthusiasm.

It might have been expected that they would have attacked and denounced it, and grasped this thistle by the hand, to uproot it from the harvest field of the world. But this is not the Divine method. God does not deal with society as a whole, but with individuals one by one ; not with the abuses, but with the spirit out of which they arise ; not with politics, but with principles. It may be that the Apostles did not realise the certain effect of the work which they did. They went quietly forward, telling out the message of God's love, reminding men that in Christ there was neither slave nor master, insisting that their true position was determined, not by their outward condition, but by their inward temper. And in doing this they were creating a world in which slavery could not live. And perhaps some who do not join in crusades against existing abuses, but concentrate all their energy to bringing individual souls from darkness to light, and from the power of Satan to God, are really doing as much as others to purify and elevate society as a whole. You will best save the world by saving the individuals who go to make it up.

Instead of denouncing slavery they borrowed from it to indicate the disposition of their lives, and interwove it into the fabric of their discourses. And so it shone with a heavenly radiance, as clouds, drenched in the glow of the setting sun, lie along the horizon as bars of gold. It is on this fact, then, that we are God's slaves, that the Apostle founds the exhortations of this paragraph.

I. THE DIVINE DESPOTISM.—This may seem a strong phrase. But it is exactly Scriptural. In the next Epistle, the word used of our Master is that from which our word "despot" was coined (2 Pet. 2: 1).[1] And it will well serve our purpose, if it startles us into a recognition of the absoluteness of Christ's authority over his own.

We are too easy in our treatment of our Lord. We call Him Master and Lord, and say well, for so He is ; but we do not realise how much the term involves ; nor do we do the things that He says. He is our Captain, and we have to go, or come, or do, not because we see the reason-ableness of His commands, but because He utters them. He is our Owner, who has purchased us for a specific purpose, and whose intentions will be frustrated unless He receive from us absolute and exact obedience. He is the Founder of our order, and surely has a right to look for as much from us as the Jesuit demands of his "black-robed militia," each of whom must be "as a staff in a blind man's hand."[2]

God hath exalted Him to be a Prince and a Saviour. We are too prone to reverse the order, and make Him a Saviour and a Prince. And we are apt to think much more of being saved by Him, than of doing as He bids. And it is because we know so little of Jesus as King that we experience so little of Him as Saviour.

It would do us good to again take the Gospels in hand, and carefully study them with the one object of noticing their incessant appeals for obedience. Everything in Christian life hinges on doing as we are told.

> *"Ours not to reason why,*
> *Ours not to make reply,*
> *Ours but to do and die."*

The rights of Jesus Christ to exercise this despotic authority are founded on many considerations, on which just now we may not dwell at length. He gave Himself for us; and his supreme gift of Himself for us demands the absolute surrender of ourselves to Him. The blood which He shed on Calvary is the price by which we have been bought; and we cannot be other than the property of our purchaser. His rights over us are also founded on the gift made by the Father to the Son, before all worlds, of those who, in the process of time, should come to Him. Besides all which, we have ourselves knelt at his feet professing our desire to be, ever, only, always his; not in part, but in the entire range of spirit, soul, and body. Who then can challenge his right to be despotic? Because He is what He is, in dignity, in character, in infinite grace, in superior knowledge, we may gladly and safely put the entire control of our lives into his hands, yielding an obedience which we dare not give to any creature living, and obeying absolutely, blindly, dumbly.

II. THE EFFECT OF THIS CONCEPTION.—"Submit." See how absolutely the Apostle rivets the collar of obedience on the necks of these scattered saints. They might be disposed to hesitate in their submission to every ordinance of man; but he silences their remonstrances, and makes their yoke easy, by whispering, *Submit, for the Lord's sake*. They might demand why they should go on in patient well-doing amid the detraction and ignorant opposition of foolish men; but he forecloses every objection, by saying, *So is the will of God*. They might vaunt their freedom, as having been introduced into a new realm, the tidings of which were beginning to steal through the world, as the first faint breath of spring through the woods: but he met their argument by reminding them that, though they were free, they must not use their liberty as a veil for evil living, because they were *the servants* (lit. *the slaves*) *of God*.

There are wonderful contrasts in these words. Those who stand erect as the brothers of Christ in the presence of God, are bidden to submit to every ordinance of men. Those who avow the determination to live only in the will of God discover that will working through the appointments of foolish and ignorant men. The freemen of God are his slaves; and therefore the servants of men. So great, and full, and rich is that real life which we may live in communion with God, that we can afford to be very liberal in complying with the demands of the human institutions by which we are surrounded, so far as they do not clash with our allegiance to our Master and Lord.

There is great helpfulness in these words. Often, when submission is required of us to some arbitrary and imperious command, we are inclined to resent it: the blood flushes our face, lightning flashes in our eyes, and we are disposed to go off in a rage, saying, "Why should I do this thing?" Then the Master approaches us, saying, "Submit for my sake; do it because I wish it: gently remonstrate against the injustice if you will, and if your remonstrances are likely to avail; but if you cannot alter or amend it, be content to submit: I wish it to be so." This makes the sullen iron swim; changes Marah into Elim; and fills the lion with the sweetness of the honeycomb. Oh, do not complain, and fret, and chafe against men! Tell your griefs to your King. Wait patiently for Him; and He will set you free. Or, if not, then believe that his permissions are his appointments; and in bending

82

your meek neck to the unwelcome yoke or human ordinances, be sure that you are performing his good pleasure.
The talisman of victory in all such cases—the key to
earth's best peace as it is to heaven's choicest boons—
is found in the little words, *"For the Lord's sake."*

There is a great reasonableness in these words. The
world from the first hated the religion of Jesus, and professed to suspect it, as inimical to itself. It was a favourite
charge against the early Christians that they were plot-
ting the overthrow of the Empire, and the dethronement
of Cæsar, in favour of "one Jesus." Their private meetings were supposed to be convened for unlawful political
purposes. It was therefore necessary that men's minds
should be disabused of the impression that any violence
subversive of existing society was contemplated.

For this purpose the early Christians were specially exhorted to conform, so far as they could, to the demands
and usages of the people amongst whom they sojourned
as pilgrims and strangers. They were to render to Cæsar
the things that were Cæsar's. If they accepted the order,
and safety, and privileges of a settled national and cor-
porate life, they were to bear their quota of its cost,
and yield homage to the form of government which they
found in vogue, agreeing to modify or alter it only by
orderly and constitutional methods. They were therefore
called upon to render to all their dues, tribute to whom
tribute, custom to whom custom, fear to whom fear,
honour to whom honour. A quiet and peaceable life
was to be their model; submission their law; well-doing
their purpose. Thus, in the process of time, they would
disarm prejudice, and conciliate their foes, by the ex-
hibition of the graces of an inoffensive, tender, and
beneficent life.

It is very beautiful to remark how literally these precepts were obeyed. Tertullian contrasts the early Christians with the heathen. These delighted in the bloody
gladiatorial shows of the amphitheatre, whereas a Christian was excommunicated if he went to it at all. When
the pagans deserted their nearest relatives in the plague,
Christians ministered to the sick. When Gentiles left their
dead unburied on the field of battle, and cast their
wounded into the streets, the disciples hastened to relieve their sufferings. Thus they *muzzled* the ignorance
of foolish men. The tide began to turn. The more *micro-
scopic* (ver. 12) was the inspection of the world, the more
evident was it that a new and blameless character was

abroad. Pliny admitted in his letter to the Emperor Trajan that there was no cause of blame in the followers of the new religion, "save a perverse and extravagant superstition." And the holy example of the primitive believers is cited by Merivale as one of the four causes of the conversion of the Roman empire.

But, of course, there are limits to the application of these words.—Our first service must always be to God. And when the demands of the king to his governors clash with the commands of the Supreme, there is no longer place for submission, but for refusal. Instantly the soul recognises that there is no room for vacillation. Indecision is not to be thought of. The Apostles, who were the first to advocate obedience to existing authority, were also the very first to exclaim, when that authority was intruding into the realm of conscience: "We must obey God rather than men." And they accepted the consequences to the bitter dregs.

The two kingdoms need not clash. We may obey God in submitting to the ordinances of men. We may do well in Cæsar's empire, without contravening our allegiance to Christ. Nay, more, we shall be better citizens to Cæsar, because we are citizens of the kingdom of heaven. But when Cæsar steps over the line of material and outward into the spiritual and eternal, there must be persistent refusal, though we rot in gaol as a consequence. But even then we are God's freemen, because his slaves.

III. THE FOURFOLD APPLICATION. *Honour all men.* Perhaps *value* or *esteem* would better render the force of the original word. They were to manifest such a kindly interest in all men as would arise from a recognition of the worth of each. There is some worth in the most worthless. In èach human being there is something which, in the eye of God, is of infinite value: a lost money-piece which has rolled away into the dust, but is worth sweeping the house to find. Put the most degraded in one scale, and the weight of a world of gold in the other, and the world would kick the beam. The blood of the Son of God is its only equivalent. Let us try to view men as God does, so shall we fulfil this injunction.

Love the brotherhood.—Love is not sentiment, but self-sacrifice ; not liking every one necessarily, but making others, instead of self, the pivot of our living. And this is the spirit which we should show to all who own the same Fatherhood, and therefore belong to the same Brotherhood.

Fear God.—True love expels the fear that hath torment, and begets godly fear that dreads to cause Him pain. And every step of growth in holiness is measured by the increase of this fear, as the rise of the Nile is measured by the breadth of territory over which it spreads itself. "Love persuades a man," says Leighton, "purely for the goodness and loveliness of God, to fear to offend Him, though there were no interest at all in it of a man's own personal misery or happiness."

Honour the king.—Respect human institutions. That lesson lay at the beginning of this paragraph, and it is repeated at its close; and, surely, if so much is said of honour for an earthly monarch, much more might be urged on the behalf of the claims of the King of kings. Oh that men would honour Him, with the honour they give to the Father! He is worthy to receive the power, and riches, and wisdom, and might, and honour, and glory, and blessing; for He was slain, and has redeemed us to God by his blood. Let us honour Him with no stinting love.

Those who give themselves most absolutely to God, are given back by Him most completely to live for others. Christ does make us members of another sphere; but at the same time He bids us, for His sake, to take a warm and living interest in all that touches human life around.

---

[1] δεσπότην—"Lord" (*Master* in R.V.). See also 2 Tim. 2:21; Jude 4; Rev. 6:10.

[2] Dr. Maclaren.

14

TAKING THINGS PATIENTLY

"What glory is it, if, when ye be buffeted for your faults, ye shall take it patiently? but if, when ye do well, and suffer for it, ye take it patiently, this is acceptable with God."—1 PETER 2:20.

The *servants* here addressed were the household servants and slaves, so largely employed in the great establishments of that age. Wealth and position made special boast of the vast number of dependents that were maintained. Life was held cheaply enough ; and when a slave was once purchased, he cost little to keep. The Roman empire swarmed with bondmen ; and they became her ruin.

It is not surprising that large numbers of these poor creatures fled to the shelter of the Christian Church, as the outcast seeks fire and food. There at least was liberty for the captives, and love and equality between slave and owner, master and serf. The purchase of the soul of the slave had cost the Son of God an equal amount of suffering with that He had endured for the wealthiest. The love that bent over the hut where an Onesimus sheltered, was as strong and tender as that which pleaded with a Philemon. The heaven which awaited the dying Lazarus, was as fair as that which beckoned a martyr Apostle. And so there was in the Gospel a marvellous fascination for the slave ; and if we may found any conclusion on the fact that large portions of the Epistles are addressed to them, and that some of the noblest passages are written for their special benefit, we must admit not only that they were to be found on the church rolls, but that the sacred writers entertained towards them a strong and tender sympathy.

The one message which the Spirit of God had for them, and which is so often repeated on these pages, may be gathered up in the words: *Submit ; endure ; be subject ; take it patiently.*

We must remember that they were not able to give notice and leave at their will. Wherever they could do this, without blame, and without detriment to the trust committed to them by God or man, they were at perfect liberty to do so. *"If thou mayest be made free, use it rather"* (1 Cor. 7: 21). But this was seldom possible. For the most part they had no alternative but to stay where they were till death released them. It was to such that these special exhortations came.

There is a great restlessness among employees throughout society. Servants giving notice. Young people trying to better themselves. Men changing from situation to situation. As a rule, there is not much gained, even in a worldly point of view, from successive changes. It is the steady plodding life which most quickly leads to success and comfort. Still, there is no sin in making a change, if it be not made simply from selfish motives, or with an eye to worldly advantage. When the Christian testimony had been clearly given, and perhaps clearly rejected; when our presence is rather an irritant to ungodliness than a persuasive to Christ; when we feel able to ask God clearly to open another door for us, and He has done as we request; when it is possible to take another position without compromising the interests committed to our care; when we can do better for the kingdom of Christ by a change—*then* there is assuredly no reason against it.

But in many cases, as with these household servants, there is no honourable way out of a position in which God seems to have wedged us. We may be in daily contact with grinding tyranny; with almost unbearable cruelty; with an envenomed tongue; with an irritating, captious, trying temper, never satisfied, never pleased—a child with the mother; a nurse with an invalid; an apprentice with an employer; a woman with her husband—in some position which cannot be altered, and where the obligation, once entered upon, must be borne to the end. Here then is the unfailing Divine recipe: when reviled, do not revile again; when buffeted though doing well, do not retaliate; when unjustly accused or punished, be still and take it patiently. And out of all this will come a life which shall not only be like His life who hath set us an example, but which shall also exert a remedial and saving influence on the most violent opposers of his Gospel, while it mounts up to God as an odour of a sweet smell, eliciting his smile of loving approbation.

Two lines of action are here referred to.

I. BUFFETED FOR FAULTS.—We have all made mistakes, and know what it is to be reprimanded or punished. But under such circumstances we have had no just ground for complaint: and our true policy when so situated must be not to excuse ourselves, nor to cast the blame on othes or on our circumstances; not to flash forth with indignant words; but to take it patiently—or if speaking, to confess our wrong, and ask to be forgiven.

In this the royal Psalmist has set us a memorable example. When he was slowly descending the long slope of Olivet towards the Jordan, there came out a man of the house of Saul, whose name was Shimei, "and as David and his men went by the way, he went along on

87

the hill's side over against them, and cursed as he went, and threw stones at him, and cast dust." And Abishai chafed at it, and asked permission to quench his abuse in blood. "No." said the king, "let him curse; because the Lord hath said unto him, Curse David."

It was as though he felt that his sin demanded public reprimand, and he meekly accepted the permission of God as his appointment. In such a spirit as this should we bear all buffeting which comes to us for our faults. Be still. Sit alone and keep silence. Put your mouth in the dust. Give your cheek to him that smiteth you. The Lord will not cast you off for ever; He will take you again to Himself. Only remember there is nothing to glory over in this. It is your common duty. "Let patience have her perfect work, that ye may be perfect and entire, wanting nothing."

II. BUFFETED, THOUGH DOING WELL.—Our superiors, or employers, may be froward, difficult to please, always finding fault; and, though we do our very best, we may meet with nothing but buffeting and rebuke. Still, we are to take it patiently.

There is no harm in quietly and temperately explaining the untruth or the unreasonableness of the accusation; or in showing how we have striven to do our best. When our Master was accused of casting out devils by collusion with their prince, He showed how unreasonable the charge was; and when smitten with the palm of the hand, He said: "If I have spoken evil, bear witness of the evil; but if well, why smitest thou Me?" It is open for us to give a soft answer like this; but if it do not turn away wrath, we must "take it patiently."

Be sure that your patience is not mean-spirited cowardice.—There is no virtue in that. But let it arise from conscience toward God. Offer your soul's patient endurance to God upon that altar which sanctifies the gift; and the motive which prompts the sacrifice will be precious in his sight. "This is thankworthy." "This is acceptable with God." And the Greek might bear such a rendering as this: *God says, Thank you.* Yes, so it is. If in some great house some poor servant, or if in a school some persecuted child, will dare, for God's sake, to choke back the passionate outburst of indignation, and to endure grief, suffering wrongfully, there is a thrill of delight started through the very heart of God, and from the throne God stoops to say, *Thank you.* The hero-explorer may be thanked by his country and his Queen; but the weakest and obscurest saint may receive the thanks of the Almighty.

We may cultivate this grace of patience by many considerations.—Though that particular allegation may be wrong, yet there have been many occasions in our lives when we have received more praise or thanks than were our due. Balance one against the other. And such is the evil of our hearts, that the germs of sins, which have been wrongly imputed to us, are latent, and only await the opportunity of breaking out; they would have broken out before, but for the grace of God. Besides, does not this desire to receive the praise and esteem of all betoken a very worldly heart? Why should we want human applause? If we had our deserts, instead of one buffet in life of caresses, we should have but one caress in a storm of buffetings. If the sinless, guileless Saviour was dumb as a sheep before its shearers amid the torrents of abuse that beset Him, surely it becomes *us* to be still, for there are plenty of causes for rebuke in us, to justify the worst things ever said against us, and many worse than these. Our case is like that of a criminal who had better bear quietly a sentence for a crime he has not committed, lest by too much outcry he induce investigation into a list of offences, which are not charged against him, because not known.

And in addition, let us think tenderly of the condition of our persecutors.—Alas, for them! How sad, how pitiable are they. Surely they need pity rather than wrath, mercy more than vehemence. Perhaps our uncomplaining meekness may touch them as no words of indignation would; as the sighs and agonies of the early martyrs were pricks and goads in the consciences of their persecutors, driving them to the Lord.

Moreover, it is after all but a small thing to be judged by man.—If he praise, what does it amount to? If he blame, what is it but a puff of smoke, a blank cartridge, a meteor exploding in the air? Life at the longest is short. Eternity is near, even at the doors. And the kiss of God, as we step across the threshold of his presence-chamber, will make us even thankful to have been put into such circumstances of rebuke as enabled us to win so large a reward.

And is it for a moment to be supposed that God will not vindicate us? Of course He will. "Shall not God avenge his own elect, which cry day and night unto Him? I tell you that He will avenge them speedily." "He will bring to light the hidden things of darkness." "He shall bring forth thy righteousness as the light, and thy judgment as the noonday." We can afford, then, to give place unto wrath, since He has said, "Vengeance belongeth unto me; I will recompense." Let us commit ourselves, as Jesus did, to Him who judgeth righteously, and we shall find that He will clear us and cause our enemies to bite the dust, as when Haman led Mordecai in triumph through the streets of Shushan.

III. THE INDUCEMENTS TO PATIENT ENDURANCE.

(1) *As we have already seen, God says, Thank you.* —And those thanks will be heard one day by the raptured soul, as it stands almost dazed in his presence. "When did I aught to deserve all this?" And in answer, many a trivial and forgotten incident of Christian gentleness and meekness under misrepresentation and rebuke, will be recalled. "This, soul, I beheld in thee; and it made Me glad. Welcome! and well done!"

(2) *For this we were called.*—Not to be happy, or saved, or glorified, but to suffer as Jesus suffered. He was the Master of the house, but they spat on Him, smote Him, derided and crucified Him; yet He threatened not. And we have been called to live His life. To make his meaning clear, the Apostle uses words which children could follow. When the Greek schoolmaster taught writing, he made his letters faintly, and the scholar wrote over his outlines. This is the Apostle's thought, and we have been called to repeat each line and turn and curve of the Master's life, so that the world may ever have a living copy of His life before its eyes. "Leaving an example."

(3) *We know we are on the right way for our home.* —Our Master has gone through the world, leaving traces of his path behind Him; as in the dense bush of Australia a man will blaze the trunks or snap the twigs, that those who follow may find the way. So, as we encounter hatred and rebuke—not for our misdeeds but because we belong to Christ—and are able to bear it patiently, we are sure that we are on His track; which leads down into the grave, and through it to the Resurrection lawns, and up the Ascension steeps, to the banks of the river of water of life, where they follow the Lamb whithersoever He goeth.

And is this patience possible? Not to your unaided
90

efforts; but as the gift of the God of Patience through the Holy Ghost. Thrice we are told of the patience of Jesus, who bore threat and wrong without a word of retaliatory threat. Oh, marvellous grace! And it was wrought out by Him, not for Himself alone, but for all who believe. It awaits our appropriation. Let us claim it in all moments of irritation and calumny, saying with Robert Hall, "Calm me, Lamb of God, calm me!" or whispering softly, "Thy patience, Lord!" So may God the Holy Spirit direct you into the patience of Jesus Christ!

15

THE FOOTPRINTS OF THE FLOCK

"For even hereunto were ye called: because Christ also suffered for us, leaving us an example, that ye should follow his steps: who did no sin, neither was guile found in his mouth: who, when He was reviled, reviled not again; when He suffered, He threatened not; but committed Himself to Him that judgeth righteously: who his own self bare our sins in his own body on the tree, that we being dead to sins should live unto righteousness: by whose stripes ye were healed. For ye were as sheep going astray; but are now returned unto the Shepherd and Bishop of your souls."—1 PETER 2:21—25.

Stray sheep! Can you not see them? They have broken through some narrow opening in the fence; have wandered afar to browse on the sweet grass that enticed them forth; have been scared and driven by dogs, broken into smaller and ever smaller companies, till at last they wander alone, or fall into pits, or lie feebly bleating with exposure and fatigue, the easy prey of lion or wolf. Far from the fold; torn, wounded, driven; panting with alarm; splashed and draggled with filth; certain to perish, unless rescued by the shepherd. Such were all of us. "We were as sheep going astray."

How shall we ever sufficiently adore the Good, Great, and Chief Shepherd of souls, that He did not leave us to our hapless fate, but came after us—down mountain rent, through thorny brake, over jagged flints, seeking until He found us, and laying us upon his shoulders, brought us back. We "are now returned." Safe sheltered in his fold. Listening for Him to call us by our name. Bearing his name branded on us. Not dreading to be put forth to new duties, trials, or temptations, because so sure that "when He putteth forth his own sheep, He goeth before them; and his sheep follow Him." But this following of the Shepherd and Bishop of our souls involves suffering. "Christ also suffered for us, leaving us an example, that we should follow his steps." It becomes us to mark well those footprints, as they lead down into the dark alley, ere they climb upward to the Resurrection and Ascension heights.

(1) *The sufferings incident to the common lot of men.* —"Man is born to trouble, as the sparks fly upward." "Work is but one half of life; suffering is the other. There is a hemisphere of the world in the sunshine of work; but there is another in the shadow of suffering." All suffer, either in body or soul; in themselves or their families; from what they have or have not; through the malice of their fellows; the malevolence of wicked spirits; or their own follies or mistakes.

In all such sufferings, except the last, Jesus suffered. Whatever is meant by hunger, thirst, weariness, poverty, and toil, physical weakness and suffering, bereavement with its prostrating anguish, He knew. These things are common to man. Enduring these he earns his bread. Through these his character is formed. By these he acquires the mastery of nature. And because the Lord was found in fashion as a man, He bowed his royal head to endure them. Though Maker and Monarch of all, He chose the mendicant's empty purse, the outcast's fare, the exile's bed, that no child of Adam should be able to boast of an excess or peculiarity of suffering, in the feeling of which He could not be touched. "He was made like unto his brethren."

(2) *There are also sufferings peculiar to Christ as Mediator and Saviour.*—The Apostle lays stress on these as the necessary foundation of our relationship to God. He "suffered *for* us"; and the preposition unmistakably denotes that He took upon Himself the curse and consequence of our sin, relieving us of it for evermore. And then as if to emphasise the work of mediation and substitution more emphatically, the Apostle quotes again

92

from that great evangelic prophecy of Isaiah in which the Spirit of Christ testified so clearly beforehand of the sacrificial aspect of the Redeemer's sufferings (Isa. 53).

He bore our sins.—It is a sacrificial word. As of old the Jew "leaned hard" on the head of the victim destined to die for him, and the innocent lamb bare the burden, dying beneath its load, so did Jesus bear our sins in his own body on the tree. It was not the anticipation of approaching physical torture which bowed Him so low in Gethsemane, or pressed the bloody sweat from Him, as the feet of the peasant press the grapes in the autumn vintage. It was the foreboding of the pressure of our sins. No sufferer has ever experienced sorrow like this. There has been nothing like it in the history of the ages; nor will it admit of repetition. "Once in the end of the world hath He appeared to put away sin by the sacrifice of Himself." In one of Adam's race alone has this tragedy of love been possible: that the sins of untold myriads should "meet on Him," and so be expiated and put away for evermore (Isa. 53:6, *marg.*).

We must not linger over the phrase which emphasises the gift of *his own body* to the work of our redemption. That body so purely born, which must have been a fair casket for the holy jewel it contained; which was in the Jordan waters was first identified in outward seeming with the weight of human sin, though in itself without sin; which was the very shrine and home of God, who had prepared it for Him; which was the vehicle for so many blessed words and deeds of ministry—*that* body was made a sin-offering, and, so to speak, was burnt in fire without the camp, as the bodies of the bulls and goats under the Levitical law. Nor must we stay to compare that *tree* with the wood which Isaac carried on his strong young shoulders to Moriah's brow. It is enough to know that it has taken deep root in our world, and is filling it with its spreading branches, the true tree of life, whose fruits drop on all lands, and whose leaves are for the healing of the nations.

But there is yet one consideration which claims our attention ere we pass on. Those sufferings, utterly unique and unapproachable by us, which rear themselves amid all compeers, in lonely and unapproachable grandeur, have for ever absolved us from having to bear the righteous penalty of the broken moral laws of God's government. We may have to bear the natural consequences and penalties of our wrong-doings. The converted drunkard, though forgiven and delivered from the penalty of God's wrath, will yet carry to his grave the marks and traces of his excess; though even these may be transmuted into blessings by the near presence of our Lord. Out of the eater will come forth meat, and out of the strong sweetness; but, as for the eternal, governmental, and judicial consequences of our sins, these have been borne for us, and have been exhausted in the sufferings of our blessed Lord. In the person of Jesus, the great God took them home to Himself, and put them away for ever. Because He has suffered them, we need not suffer them; because He has borne them, we need not bear them; because the stripes fell thick and heavy on Him, they need never fall on us. "By his stripes ye were healed."

The slaves whom the Apostle was addressing understood full well the meaning of "stripes." The Greek word means *the weal* left by a stripe. From the grave the Saviour came, bearing the weals of many stripes, woundmarks in hands and feet and side; but those bruises and wounds tell a story which makes our hearts leap with joy. When the Great Shepherd, raised through the blood of the everlasting covenant, met his timid followers in the upper room, He bade them behold the print of the nails, and the scar in his side. "Then were the disciples glad." And as we consider the Lamb, "as it had been slain," and discern those precious memorials of his finished work on our behalf, we too may break forth into new songs, like those in heaven. Those stripes are the price of our redemption, the evidence of our purchase, the sign-manual of pardon. Let us then appropriate these triumphant words, and the whole verse of which they form the appropriate close; and let each of us dare to say, not because we feel it, but because we accept it as the word of God, which cannot be broken: "He was wounded for my transgressions; He was bruised for my iniquities; the chastisement of my peace was upon Him; and with his stripes I am healed."

But the death of our Lord Jesus has a double aspect. —It looks first towards the justice of God, to which it rendered an adequate equivalent for our many sins. This was altogether independent of us, for whom it was given. But it also looks towards man in the effect it produces on those who rightly apprehend it. "That we, being dead to sins, should live unto righteousness." There is a remarkable coincidence of testimony between this statement and that in Rom. 5. Indeed, in these words we strike one of the main seams of Scripture teaching. In the sight of God, we are reckoned as being so identified with our Lord that what is predicted of Him is also true of us. Dead in his death. Raised in his resurrection. Seated with Him in his glory. And it should be the purpose and aim of our life to realise by faith in actual practice and experience all that is ours in the mind and purpose of God. Ye died: reckon yourselves dead. Ye are risen: set your affection on things above. Ye are seated in heavenly places: walk worthy of your high calling. By the grace of God, there should be a perpetual deadness to every appeal that comes from the flesh, the world, or the devil; and an ever fuller response to the inspirations and appeals which come from the Spirit of God to a life of righteousness.

The mediatorial sufferings of Christ do thus involve some suffering to us. Because we must submit to daily death; we must take up our cross and follow Him; we must sow ourselves, falling into the ground to die. A perpetual self-denial; a setting up of the cross in our lives; a conformity to his death; a drinking of his cup; a baptism into his sufferings—all these are the indispensable conditions of that salvation from the love and power of sin which He has wrought out for us. But in no deeper sense can we follow in his steps as the Substitute, Mediator, Reconciler, and High Priest of men.

(3) *The sufferings of the sinless Man.*—That He was sinless was universally attested. No lamb or heifer was ever so searched for blemishes as was He. Judas, who knew Christ's innermost history, declared that he had "betrayed innocent blood." Pilate repeatedly insisted that he could find no fault in Him at all. And the only charge that the priests could substantiate against Him was his assumption of Deity. "He did not sin, neither was guile found in his mouth." He did not say, Yea and Nay; but all the promises of God in Him were yea, and, through Him, amen. He was the true and faithful Witness.

And how lovely was his silence before his accusers. Silent before the Sanhedrin, whilst the false witnesses hopelessly involved themselves. Silent before Herod, so that from entering his halls to leaving them, no word escaped his lips—emblem of the silence of God to those whose natures are closed to Him. Silent before Pilate, except when that poor craven soul gave expression to thoughts and questionings which surged up from its very depths. Silent in the Palace-hall. Silent in the Prætorium. Silent on the cross, save in words of blessing and prayer.

But how inevitable it was that holiness like His, even though so still and uncomplaining, which did not strive, nor cry, nor lift up, nor cause its voice to be heard in the streets, should come into collision with the spirit of his time; and in that collision suffer bitterly! As the shining of the sun brings out the poisonous fumes of the stagnant pool, so did the presence of Jesus among men stir up the evil of human hearts; and that evil must in itself have been a cause of awful suffering to one so sensitive, so delicate, so holy as He was. The keener the appreciation of musical harmonies, the intenser must ever be the agony of a discordant note.

Sum up, if you can, the ingredients of suffering in Christ's cup. That the race with which He stood in such close identification was so steeped in sin that He was compelled to breathe our polluted atmosphere, all the more terrible, in contrast with that of the world from which He had come, as the foul miasma of a fœtid court or room is the more distressing to those who have just entered it from the fresh outer air; that He was misrepresented and misunderstood and held guilty of sins against the divinest traditions of his people; that He was treated as a madman, and as possessed of weakened intellect; that He was obliged to endure the contradictions of sinners against Himself; that He was opposed and hated by those whom He yearned to save; that He was exposed to the temptations of men and devils—are not all these footprints of suffering flecked with blood, which substantiate the frequent references of this eye-witness to the sufferings of Christ?

In all this He has left us an example that we should follow in his steps. It is inevitable that we should pass through many of the same experiences. The Christ-life in us must pass through the same stages of development and meet with the same treatment, as it did in Him. The world is not more friendly than in the long past to the Master's spirit; and in proportion as we are animated by it shall we be brought into the same collision with the spirit of human society, and suffer from its incongruity to the holiest instincts of the soul.

Expect to be reviled and buffeted, misunderstood and misrepresented, cast out and crucified, as He was. The sheep cannot expect to fare better than the Shepherd; nay, they know that they are on his track, when constrained to follow in his footprints of suffering and sorrow. But the end will be glorious, when the whole flock are gathered on the hills of eternity. If we died, we shall also live, with Him. If we suffer, we shall also reign, with Him. "Ye are they which have continued with Me in my temptations; and I appoint unto you a kingdom as my Father hath appointed unto Me."

16

WOMAN'S PLACE IN THE HOME

'Likewise, ye wives, be in subjection to your own husbands; that if any obey not the word, they also may without the word be won by the conversation of the wives: while they behold your chaste conversation coupled with fear. Whose adorning let it not be that outward adorning of plaiting the hair, and of wearing of gold, or of putting on of apparel; but let it be the hidden man of the heart, in that which is not corruptible, even the ornament of a meek and quiet spirit, which is in the sight of God of great price. For after this manner in the old time the holy women also, who trusted in God, adorned themselves, being in subjection unto their own husbands: even as Sara obeyed Abraham, calling him lord; whose daughters ye are, as long as ye do well, and are not afraid with any amazement. Likewise, ye husbands dwell with them according to knowledge, giving honour unto the wife, as unto the weaker vessel, and as being heirs together of the grace of life; that your prayers be not hindered.'—1 Peter 3:1—7.

There were pure and virtuous homes in the old classic world, of which the fragrant memory lingers to this day. Who can forget Panthea, who, as her husband left her to fight under the renowned Cyrus, said:—"If ever there was a woman that regarded her husband more than her own soul, I am that woman"? Who can forget the refusal of Cornelia to accept one of her many and even royal suitors, because she insisted that her marriage with her noble husband, Titus Gracchus, was not annulled by his death? Who will be untouched by that exquisite description from the hand of the great Pliny, who, speaking of his wife, said:—"She loves me, the surest pledge of her virtue; and adds to this a wonderful disposition to learning, which she has acquired from her love to me. She reads my writings, studies them, and even gets them by heart. You would smile to see the concern she is in when I have a cause to plead; and her joy when it is over. She finds means to have the first news brought her of the success I meet with in court. She accompanies my verses with the lute, with no master but love, the best of instructors. Her affection is not founded on my worth or person; but she is in love with the immortal part of me"?

But these were isolated instances, canonised in history because so exceptionally rare. The poets and historians of the Roman Empire paint in the blackest colours the utter disregard of the marriage tie; the abominable and shameless immorality which snapped the foundations of the State, and led with inevitable exactness to its fall. These descriptions are more than substantiated by the revelation of the walls of Pompeii. Into such a world of stygian darkness, lit by a few stars, came the religion of our Lord, and among its very first creations was that of the family and the home. For these, its earliest and most precious gifts to the age of its inception, and to all ages, mankind must ever own itself indebted to the Gospel of the Lord Jesus.

Even the Jewish people had become grossly lax in their notions of the obligations of wedded love. The rabbis permitted divorce on the most trivial pretexts. If the husband were not pleased with his wife's behaviour, or if she spoilt his food in cooking, or were stricken with a grievous bodily affliction, he might put her away. It was held indeed that this facility was a special privilege granted to Israel, but not to other nations. That such was the state of society brings into startling emphasis the words of Christ, who repeatedly went back to the primeval institution of marriage, one woman for one man, and insisted that these two must live together in the home, in a relationship which could only be dissolved by death or by unfaithfulness.

It is necessary that these words of Christ and his Church should again speak in the ears of the world. The growing revolt of the classes and the masses from the simplicities of Christianity is being followed closely by an increasing disregard of the ties of marriage and the bonds of home.

How rapidly the business of the divorce courts is increasing. We must have, forsooth, looser divorce laws. We must not be too puritanic. We must admit with Strauss that the New Testament contains "ascetic" notions concerning marriage; that the Sermon on the Mount is deficient in the knowledge of human nature; that the scientific method is in collision with the Biblical ideal. And we are asked to condone the offences of certain great thinkers and brilliant writers of our time against the sacrament of marriage, as if their genius relieved them of moral obligation, or put them under some special *régime.*

From such lamentable laxity, which is doing so much to dislodge from its position the key-stone of our national greatness, little heeding the lessons of the past, or realising the full measure of disaster which must crown the success of its endeavours we turn with relief to the high, pure, and divine conception of the place of woman in the Christian hame, her adorning, and her treatment.

I. HER POSITION.—It is true that she is bidden to be in subjection. But then we must also remember the peculiar circumstances under which these Epistles were written and the revolution which was afoot.

Women had been degraded for centuries, as they are degraded now throughout the Orient, and where Christianity has not come—supposed to be destitute of souls; the drudge and slave, or toy; a piece of property, valuable or not, as the case might be. But, like a ray of dawn, there came the teaching of the Gospel. Woman was declared to be the helpmate of man, taken not from his head or feet, but from his side, to be his companion. In Christ was neither male nor female. The Holy Spirit showed no partially in his operations, but endowed the women of the early Church equally with the men. The Lord Himself had admitted women to the inner circle of his blessed friendship, and had called out their noblest attributes. Before the eyes of the world there hung the memory of the Virgin Mother; of the woman who ministered to Him; of those who broke their alabaster boxes on his person; of those who were last at his cross, first at his grave. The miracle at the peasants' marriage was a sign of the Master's smile on this holy rite. And, as these visions passed before the retina of woman's heart, she responded to the call of Jesus with glad delight; she flung herself at his feet with the rapturous cry, "Rabboni"; she pressed into his Church, where she was welcome; and there was a danger lest in the new-found ecstasy she might break loose from those sacred obligations which were as old as Paradise, and which no Gospel could sever or relax. Christ had not come to destroy the primeval rite, but to fulfil, and to show that it was a pattern of that eternal and indissoluble union into which He enters with his Church.

This was the origin of the command to be in subjection. It was, primarily, addressed to those who since their marriage had become Christians. There was considerable hesitancy in the early Church, as to their duty under such circumstances. "Should they leave their husbands?" "Should they alter their behaviour to them?" "Should they assume any superiority?" "No," said the Apostles, "stay where you are, however painful your position, and uncongenial your surroundings, and trying your husband's conduct. Be chaste, gentle, loving, submissive, winsome, so that hearts may be softened, which have never heard a word of Gospel preaching, and may be won by the beauty of your holy and unselfish lives."

Of course, where true love subsists between husband and wife, and where both are Christians, such a command as this is hardly needed. There is no room for subjection, where there are no masterful commands; no standing up for rights; no jealous strife for independence. The sensitive instincts of love define exactly, as no words could do, the respective position of husband and wife; and, altogether apart from such an injunction as this, it is perhaps rather the nature of woman's love to yield, to lean on one stronger than itself, and to give itself away in deeds of loving ministry.

If all Christian women would live like this, there would be less need of preaching to their unconverted husbands. "Without a word, they would be won by the conversation of their wives." Won! "A soul converted is gained to itself, gained to the pastor or friend or wife or husband who sought it, and gained to Jesus Christ; added to his treasury, who thought not his own precious blood too dear to lay out for this gain." And what more precious guerdon could reward a wife's chaste and God-fearing behaviour than to know that her husband was to be a jewel in her crown, won for her Lord!

There is nothing here for those who desire to marry out of the Lord. They are clearly forbidden to be unequally yoked with unbelievers; and they will find, to their cost, how bitter a thing it is to disobey a distinct command. No hope is held out of either winning the other, where from the first God's Word has been set at nought. But where conversion has taken place after marriage in the case of one partner, there is every reason to cherish hope for the other.

Oh, brokenhearted women, disappointed and of sorrowful spirit, ready to despair, disposed to abandon heart and hope, be not weary in well-doing; be yours the love that never faileth; remember that, in dark places, you are to exemplify that love for the sake of the dear Master, who is looking on and will not let you be tempted beyond what you are able to bear; dare to trust Him for the future, and believe that God will yet give you your dearest who sails in the ship with you over the stormy waves.

What a lesson is here for all! We cannot all preach by lip; but we can by life. And such preaching is mighty in results; whilst the effect of it abides long after the life has passed from view into the ministries of the upper sanctuary.

II. HER ADORNING.—It does not seem that the Apostle forbids plaiting the hair, or wearing of gold, any more than he does the putting-on of apparel. Religion does not consist in the presence or absence of these things. If we wear them, we are not better; if we abjure them, we are not worse. It makes surely very little difference to the Saviour whether we dress in silk or calico, in colours or drab. The one law is—to dress as becomes the station in which He has placed us, and in such a way as not to attract notice to ourselves.

Of course if a certain style of dress is associated only with the worldy and irreligious; or if it exercises an injurious effect on those who minutely watch and exaggerate what they see in us; or if it attracts excessive remark, and makes us selfconscious—we do well to discard it, and lay it aside. But where this is not the case, it is well to keep moderately in the wake of custom and usage, lest we attract as much attention by our prudery as our pride, and so minister to our accursed love of singularity. But it is very pitiful when the Christian conscience becomes morbid on these points. Some are so constantly questioning what dress their Lord would have them wear, that they miss much of his company. Of course, we ought to select our attire under his eye, asking for his guidance in our choice, and his grace to indicate his taste for us.

Surely the Master has a right to say what his slaves should wear, and how they should spend this money! And He will indicate his will in the gentlest and most delicate manner. Cast the responsibility more utterly on Him, and then occupy yourselves much more with Himself than with your attire, so occupied with Him as to be almost oblivious of it.

The great point with each of us should be: *Where is my adorning?"* If it be without, then indeed we are in evil case. But if it be within—in the hidden man of the heart, in the cultivation of a meek and quiet spirit—we may leave outward matters to shape themselves very much as they may; and they will cease to attract an undue share of our attention or thought. Great is he, says Seneca, who enjoys his earthenware as if it were plate; and not less great is the man to whom all his plate is no more than earthenware. Plenty are there whose outward body is richly decked, but whose inner being is clothed in rags; whilst others, whose garments are worn and threadbare, are all glorious within. It is a solemn question: What are our garments in the sight of God? Do we know anything of this meek and quiet spirit, so precious in his esteem, so restful and blessed amid the tumult of the world?

The clue to its possession seems hidden in the suggestion *that the holy women in the old time trusted in God.* Turn your heart towards God; and the result will show itself in such wholesomeness of behaviour, such consistency in well-doing, such freedom from sudden fear, as will commend the Gospel, and attract the smile of God.

III. HER TREATMENT.—These words to husbands may well be extended by the addition of the words spoken to them in the Epistle to the Ephesians, in which they are bidden to love their wives as Christ has loved the Church, nourishing and cherishing them as their own body.

But three striking and beautiful suggestions are made here which will suffice: —

(1) *Give honour to the wife as the weaker vessel.*—All bear on their nature the touch of the great Potter's moulding hand; but some are stronger than others, and in Christ's code the obligation to consider the other always rests with the stronger. Politeness, high-breeding, chivalry, courtesy—these are mimicked in society; but their original

types are found only where Christianity has wrought her perfect work. No man can fully acquire them until this Gospel is written in his heart; they pass from within outwards, not from without inwards. And many who have never been admitted to so-called good society are God's own gentlepeople.

(2) *Remember that you are heirs together of the grace of life.*—There is no such union as that of those who are wedded in the love of God, and to whose love his love gives depth and meaning and a touch of infinitude. Of a relationship like this we may well repeat the motto on Charles Kingley's grave, summing up a life of exquisite married bliss: *we love; we loved; we will love.* Let thoughts of the common grace of life temper and ennoble your relations.

(3) *See that your prayers be not hindered.*—There is no test so subtle as a good man's prayers. When he kneels before his God, He will know in a moment whether or not he has contracted defilement during the preceding hours; and, if so, where. And he is bidden to leave his gift at the altar, and go to seek reconciliation, ere he returns to offer it. Whatever then arises in the hour of prayer, and breathes on the mirror of the heart, is thereby proved to be injurious and wrong, and must be put away. Whatever makes husband and wife unable to pray together alone, or at the family altar, must be dealt with mercilessly as a hindrance. And if only we are faithful and true in these daily particulars of conduct, our prayers will not only be unhindered but helped, and we shall gain such conceptions of the love of Christ to us, amid all our failures and imperfections, as will make the wedding bells ring out a perpetual chime of love within our hearts, and we shall understand another phase of his love which passeth knowledge.

There is nothing which tests us so much as the daily discipline of the home life. It is much easier to stand amid a crowded assembly calling Christians to entire consecration, than, on the following morning, to bring those lofty principles to bear on the small details of the breakfast-table, when the radiant light of the Transfiguration Mount has been exchanged for the grey of an autumn day-break, and the excitement of the crowds for the simple presence of wife and child. It is not so difficult to live like saints where we are set free from the ordinary friction and responsibilities of daily life, and surrounded by those who interpose as many pillows of loving consideration as possible between us and anything which would fret and annoy us. At the same time, if our religion breaks down here it breaks down utterly. If we are not right, so far as in us lies, with our nearest, it is very questionable if we are right with God. Love to God involves love to man. And if we do not love with a warm, sunny, attractive, and unselfish love those who live within our home circle, we may gravely question whether we have tasted of the love of God. For even if we have come to the end of our love we may become the channels through which His love may flow down to bless and save.

17

THE CHRISTIAN TEMPER

"Finally, be ye all of one mind, having compassion one of another; love as brethren; be pitiful; be courteous; not rendering evil for evil, or railing for railing; but contrariwise blessing; knowing that ye are thereunto called, that ye should inherit a blessing. For he that will love life. and see good days, let him refrain his tongue from evil, and his lips that they speak no guile: Let him eschew evil, and do good; let him seek peace, and ensue it. For the eyes of the Lord are over the righteous, and his ears are open unto their prayers: but the face of the Lord is against them that do evil."—1 PETER 3:8—12.

In his life of Frederick the Great, Carlyle describes in a few graphic touches the Moravian town of Herrnhut; and, after remarking on the religious atmosphere which brooded over the place, he says, "Herrnhut is a Sabbath petrified; a Calvinistic Sabbath done into stone." It is a high eulogium. But every visitor to that unique settlement has been arrested by the careful accuracy with which the principles of their religion and theology have been exemplified to the minutest details in the lives of its inhabitants.

But it were a still greater marvel to find in any community under heaven a complete embodiment of these marvellous injunctions. All of one mind; cemented into a holy unity by a common sympathy. Ministering to the saints. Pitiful to the weak, erring, and poor. Courteous to equals. Calm and forgiving under abuse and injury. Seeking peace. Living under the smile of God. Where in all the world can we discover such a community of Christians? It were a fair vision, worth going far to see. A temple to Love. An abode of heavenly bliss. An oasis in the desert. A snatch of celestial harmony amid the jarring discords of human selfishness. The New Jerusalem descending from God out of heaven. Yet nothing less than this is the Christian ideal, as it is also that which our Lord died to secure. And it would well become us, if, without waiting for others, each one would adopt the injunctions of these verses as the binding rule and regulation of daily life. This would be our worthiest contribution to the convincing of the world, and to the coming of the kingdom of our Lord. And it would spread.

And does not the Apostles' use of the word *finally* teach us that all Christian doctrine is intended to lead up to and inaugurate that life of love, the bold outlines of which are sketched in these words? Let us not be content with considering the mighty stones of truth laid by this wise Master Builder in the foundations; but let us pass up, and into the temple based upon them, where the shekinah dwells above the mercy-seat, so that we may catch its glow upon our faces, and bear it forth into the world.

I. THE GENERAL PRINCIPLE.—"Be ye all of one mind, having compassion one of another." This oneness of mind does not demand the monotony of similarity, but unity in variety. Not the oneness of a hop-pole, or of a pile of hop-poles; but of the plant which, with tendril, leaf, and fruit, rears itself aloft in the summer air. Not the oneness of a brick, or of a pile of bricks; but of the house, in which so many different materials and contrivances combine to shelter human life. Not the oneness of a child; but of a family of children who differ in age, character, temperament, and chosen pursuits, but are one in love and tender sympathy.

We shall never be of one mind in the sense of all holding the same opinions; but we may be all of one mind when, beneath diversities of opinion, expression, and view, we are animated by a common devotion to Christ; a common loyalty to the great underpinning *facts* of Redemption; and a common love to all who hold the

Head, though they may differ from us in an infinite variety of minor considerations.

The Church of Rome never caught this idea. Its only conception of the oneness of Christ's disciples was a vast uniformity, a system in which every one should utter the same formularies, worship in the same postures, and belong to the same ecclesiastical order. And its leaders did their best to realise their dream. They sought to exterminate divergence of view by fire, and sword, and torture. They spread their network through the world. And just before the dawn of the Reformation they seemed to have succeeded. At the beginning of the sixteenth century, Europe reposed in the monotony of almost universal uniformity under the almost universal supremacy of the Papacy. Rome might almost have adopted the insolent boast of the Assyrian of prophecy: "As one gathereth eggs, so have I gathered all the earth ; and there was none that moved the wing, or opened the mouth, or peeped." And what was the result? There is but one answer possible. *The deep sleep of death*. And it must always be so. Life abhors uniformity. And whenever you force this marvellous being into your castiron mould, you not only destroy its grace and beauty, but you kill it.

There is variety in *the human body,* from eyelash to foot, from heart to blood disc, from brain to quivering nerve fibre ; yet in all this variety each one is conscious of an indivisible unity. There is variety in *the tree*: the giant arms that wrestle with the storm, the far-spreading roots that moor it to the soil, the myriad leaves through which the winds make music, the cones or nuts which it flings on the forest floor ; yet in all this it is one. There is variety in *the Bible*—variety of authorship, of style, of age, from the bulrush ark to the break of the sapphire waves of the Ægean about Patmos ; yet for all this the sixty-six tractlets which compose the Bible are always bound up in one cover, because composing one book. So with *Christians*. There may be, and must be, infinite varieties, and shades of thought and work ; but, notwithstanding all, there is a oneness which needs not to be created, for it is already consummated, but which must be recognised and kept. "Endeavouring to keep the unity of the Spirit in the bond of peace." Many folds, but one flock. Many stones, but one breastplate. Many temperaments, but one family. Many minds, but one mind.

Much of the controversy of the present day arises from failure to recognise the almost infinite variety of the human mind. No two persons look at the same thing in the same way, or give the same version of an incident or a tale. Each colours it with the tint of personal idiosyncrasy, just as each object in nature borrows from sunlight its special hue. Start a dozen devout, deeply-taught men to formulate any doctrine of the faith; whilst each holds the fact, no two will express it in precisely the same way. We must distinguish between *facts* and *views of facts*. Men may not think alike, and yet be of the same mind.

If we would obey this injunction of being "all of one mind," let us think more often of the things in which we agree than of those in which we differ. All are loved with the same love; bought by the same blood; born of the same Spirit; members of the same body; animated by the same life; subject to the same hopes and fears, afflictions and vicissitudes; drawing our daily sustenance from the same supplies; destined for the same home. How many and close are the bonds of our relationship! Surely it becomes us to have great compassion one toward another: correcting each other, if need be, privately or before the Church. with no desire for self-exhaltation, but with eager loyalty for the glory of God; putting the best construction on points of difference; viewing everything in the light of the Master's glory; and trying to be more animated by that loving, tender, compassionate spirit, which enabled Him to bear so long with the misunderstanding, strife, and stupidity, of the men whom He had chosen to form the inner circle of his earthly life.

II. FOUR SPECIFIC APPLICATIONS.—(1) *To fellow-Christians. Love as brethren.*—"Love" is not identical with "like." Providence does not ask us whom we would *like* to be our brethren—that is settled for us; but we are bidden to love them, irrespective of our natural predilections and tastes. You say—That is impossible. But remember that true love does not necessarily originate in the emotions, but in the will; it consists not in feeling, but in doing; not in sentiment, but in action; not in soft words, but in noble and unselfish deeds.

Love changes the pivot and centre of life from self to another. Before she flings her magic spell upon us, we are self-contained and self-centred, bending all our energies to our self-aggrandisement, compelling all streams to flow into the Dead Sea of our own interest. But when we love, a marvellous transformation passes over us.

We think more often of the beloved than of ourselves. We find our plans, contrivings, activities, all ennobled and transfigured by our one consideration of what will please and help and bless that choice spirit which has gathered to itself the threads of our life, weaving them after its own sweet will, and threading them with blessedness, as black-lettered pages may be illumined by scrolls of gold and colour. With such love should we love our fellow-Christians.

Do not begin with trying to love every one at once. We do not best descend from generals to particulars; but ascend from particulars to generals. Begin with those nearest to you in the church and the home, or in the little religious *coterie* with which you are wont to mix. It is through the love of individuals that we come to love the whole.

You say that this is your difficulty, and that there are Christians in your immediate circle, whom you cannot get on with. Here, then, is my advice. Do not try to feel love, but *will* to love. Tell the dear Master that you are willing to love, or willing to be made willing to love, but that He must create the grace of love within your breast. Ask Him to pour the tides of his love through your heart, that He may love through you; and you shall finally catch the glow and grace of his tenderness. Offer Him your lips, that by them He may speak the words you cannot utter; and your hand, that by it He may do the gentle deeds of ministry which you cannot bring yourself to perform. Your confessions of inability will bring out the assurances of his all-sufficiency. What you cannot do, He can and will do through you. All things are possible to Him. and will be to you if you believe in Him. Begin, then, to do what you know you ought to do, and would do, if you felt love. Do it because it is right; do it for Christ's sake; do it expecting the Lord to work in and through you—and you will find ere long that streams of Divine tenderness have commenced to flow through the channels of your being, long choked with silt and débris. And love thus practically learnt to one fellow-believer, will open your heart to all.

(2) *To the weak and erring. Be pitiful!*—Oh for the compassion of our blessed Lord! How often it breaks out in the Gospel narrative to the unshepherded sheep, to the hungry multitudes, and to the afflicted who sought his aid! It is so much easier to scourge, rebuke, criticise, and condemn, than to pity and heal. We must not con-

done sin, or allow ourselves to think lightly of that which has cost God so much, and which is the object of his wrath. But we may discriminate between sin and the sinner, between disease and the sufferer; and, whilst we give no quarter to the one, we may be very merciful to the other.

Think of thine own sins. How near thou hast been to the precipice, how much thou owest to the grace of God! The measure of thy debt was ten thousand talents; but it has been freely forgiven. And thy provocation to sin may have been less urgent, thy passions less fiery, thy opportunities less frequent, thy temper less persistent. And who can estimate the blackness of darkness in which the transgressor is tossed, despair at the helm, whilst the waves rush past to break in thunder on the rocks close by! Such may be the lot of one near thee! Be pitiful! Consider thyself, lest thou also be tempted. Refrain speech and action till thou knowest all.

(3) *To equals. Be courteous!*—The courtesies of Christianity should be more inward and constant than those of the world. Be ready to take the least comfortable seat, to move up to the end of the pew, or to give up your comfortable corner. Do not sit down at the extreme end of a meeting-room, compelling late-comers to have the discomfort of passing to the front before the eyes of all, much to the distraction of the leader. Let others sit while you stand. Do not push and crowd as you come in or go out. Step back to let women and children and invalids pass by. Let the manners of your Father's court be always evident in your deportment, that men may feel that you come of a noble line, and learn that Christianity produces not simply the heroism of a great occasion, but the thousand minute courtesies of daily living.

(4) *To enemies. Do not retaliate!*—"Not rendering evil for evil, but contrariwise blessing." The old law of "an eye for an eye" is repealed, in favour of that nobler legislation which bids us do good to those that hate us, and pray for them who despitefully use and persecute us. Let us be like the rock on the wilderness march, which when smitten yielded water to the thirsty hosts.

We can afford to do this; for we have been called to inherit such a blessing that, though we give it away with both hands, in spendthrift prodigality, we can never exhaust it. Besides, this is the policy of living a calm, good, and blessed life. He that loves life, and would see good days, must keep his tongue from evil, and his lips from guile. The man who is always vindicating himself and standing up for his rights, will be perpetually in a ferment, and will miss the cream of life, which rises when all is still. But, better than all, our God will see to us, protecting and delivering us. Not a blow reaches us which He does not notice. Not a threat which He does not hear. He will put an arrest on the enemy when his purpose is accomplished. And then, from out the cloud, He will look upon the armies of our foes, and discomfort them, and overthrow them in the heart of the sea. "His face is against them that do evil."

18

SUFFERING FOR RIGHTEOUSNESS' SAKE

"Who is he that will harm you, if ye be followers of that which is good? But and if ye suffer for righteousness' sake, happy are ye: and be not afraid of their terror, neither be troubled; but sanctify the Lord God in your hearts: and be ready always to give an answer to every man that asketh you a reason of the hope that is in you, with meekness and fear: having a good conscience; that whereas they speak evil of you, as of evil-doers, they may be ashamed that falsely accuse your good conversation in Christ. For it is better, if the will of God be so, that ye suffer for well-doing than for evil-doing."— 1 PETER 3:13—17.

Twice in this paragraph we meet the word *suffer;* and in each case it is associated with that special kind of suffering which is inflicted on the innocent and holy by those who hate the light flung in on their own darkness, and who desire to extinguish it if they may.

The incarnation led inevitably to the cross. Any attentive student of human nature who stood with Jesus on the threshold of his life, and heard Him speak or saw Him act, must have been convinced that there was but one fate reserved for such a one as He was. And though the acts of love and power which marked his busy days—as the silver bells which made music at every

110

movement of Israel's high priest—averted the crisis for some few months, it came; as from the first it was evident that it must come. Amid every sign of vehement hatred, the Lamb of God was led to his death; hurried out of the world as millions of his followers have been since. From Bethlehem the road lay straight to Calvary.

And what was true of the Son of God in his human flesh is true of each incarnation of Him in our hearts and lives. Where, by the Holy Spirit, He enters into the nature of those who consecrate themselves wholly to Him, and begins to live freely and mightily within them, He will not only manifest much of the grace and power of his own human life, but He will also come into collision with the prejudices and interests of worldly and evil men, incurring as of old their most virulent dislike, and probably their violent resistance.

THE ORIGIN OF PERSECUTION.—We cannot analyse at length all *the causes of the inevitable dislike* which the world feels towards the Christian. They are many, and obvious. For instance: *The man of God should be an embodied conscience*. The one endeavour of ungodly men is to drown the remonstrances of conscience. For this they plunge into gaiety, or business, or exploration; for this they hurry from scene to scene; for this they studiously avoid all that savours of God or his claims. But in a holy life they meet with a devout and constant recognition of those claims, coupled with a faithful endeavour to fulfil them. There is an embodiment of righteousness without them, which arouses into instant and unwelcome activity those convictions of their duty which they have done their best to quell. There is the pride of heart which resents superiority in another. There is the envy which grudges the influence that goodness always attracts. There is the malice which broods over the contrast that purity presents to impurity, until the fact of its doing so bulks as a positive injury. All these strong passions of the unrenewed heart, like Pilate and Herod of old, become friends in their common antagonism to the saintliness which intrudes upon their privacy and menaces their peace.

Besides, there is always *an aggressiveness in true Christianity* which arouses strong resistance. We readily admit that, in one aspect, it does not strive, nor cry, nor lift up, nor cause its voice to be heard. Soft as the zephyr which scarcely stirs the bearded wheat; light as the tread of the morning; gentle as distilling dew-drops—does the religion of Jesus spread onwards over the world. And yet it endangers crafts; undermines profitable but nefarious trades; steals away customers from the devil's shrines; attacks vested interests; and turns the world upside down. A tiresome, annoying, gain-sapping thing is pure and undefiled religion; and the devil's servants have a bad time of it when the Puritan reigns, or the Revival sweeps as a prairie fire through the community. "If we let Him alone, all men will believe on Him; and the Romans will come and take away both our place and nation."

Have we not here the clue to the subsidence of persecution in our days? True, each age has its peculiar discipline; and ours is cursed by a soft, luxurious worldliness, which is most hostile to the manifestation of strong and heroic principle. But is not there too great a contrast between our lives and those of our forefathers? Where is the saintliness of living, the zeal for souls, the uncompromising rebuke of evil, the sturdy adherence to principle at all costs, which littered the Alpine summits with the bones of slaughtered saints, and lit the fires of Smithfield? If these virtues were more generally embodied in the daily practice of the majority, as they are in that of a small minority of professing Christians, can there be much doubt as to the issue? Men might not adopt the barbarous expedients of former days, for even in this they unconsciously do homage to Jesus of Nazareth; but they would find some other method of ridding themselves of the unwelcome protests of holy lives against the selfishness and evil of their own condition.

Ah, it is one of the most terrible rebukes that Incarnate Love can administer, when it says of any now, as it did of some in the days of his flesh: "The world cannot hate you." Not to be hated by the world; to be loved and flattered and caressed by the world—is one of the most terrible positions in which a Christian can find himself. "What bad thing have I done," asked the ancient sage, "that he should speak well of me?" The absence of the world's hate proves that we do not testify against it that its works are evil. The warmth of the world's love proves that we are of its own. The friendship of the world is enmity with God. Whosoever therefore will be a friend of the world is the enemy of God (John 7·7; 15:19; James 4:4).

THE BLESSEDNESS OF THE PERSECUTED.—"Blessed are ye."
A beatitude caught from the lips of Jesus, and ringing but
again in our next chapter (Matt. 5:10 and 1 Pet. 4:14).
Blessedness is a higher thing than happiness, and is consistent with the most trying circumstances. But what a
universal testimony has been given to that blessedness
shining from the faces and breathing from the lips of
those who have suffered for righteousness' sake!

A recent writer has culled the words from dying martyr-
testimonies; and they testify to this inner blessedness.
"I was glad when they said unto me, Let us go into the
house of the Lord," said one martyr, as he was condemned to die.

> *"This prison very sweet to me*
> *Hath been since I came here;*
> *And so would also hanging be,*
> *If Thou didst then appear,"*

sang Bunyan in Bedford Gaol, his eyes dazzled with
frescoes painted by angel hands on the damp walls. "Methinks they strew roses at my feet," said another, as the
faggots were lighted about him.

And wherein does this blessedness consist? It comes
through the inner possession by the spirit of that heavenly
temper, which is inspired by the Spirit of God, and is
close akin to Him, and is in itself blessedness. It comes
through the enforced constraint laid upon the soul to
seek its delight and rapture in the love and friendship
of Christ, the Friend of the persecuted, who is always
nearest to those who are most like Him in suffering,
because most like in character and life. It comes through
the glad consciousness of being on the path trodden
already by prophets and righteous men, who have gone
through flood and flame, but who have overcome, and
are set down with Christ on his throne. It comes because
the exceeding great reward beckons from on high.

There are many gates into blessedness. It stands four-
square; and, judging from our Lord's words, it has two
gateways on each side, so that no life is so far away
or obscure, but it may enter in and dwell there. Choose
you which gate you will! And if you are not able to lay
claim to poverty of spirit, or mercifulness, or purity in
heart, then dare to do well at all costs; pursue patiently
the path of lofty integrity and blameless purity; bear the
suffering which will inevitably fall to your lot with un-

113

complaining patience and fortitude—and there will be administered to you a blessed and abundant entrance into that kingdom of blessedness which is already established on earth, standing with its sapphire walls and gates amid the erections of men, unstained by their pollutions, as it is unseen by any but purged eyes. "If ye suffer for righteousness' sake, blessed are ye."

THE BEHAVIOUR OF THE PERSECUTED.—(1) *Be not afraid.* There seems here a reminiscence on Peter's part of words heard long before: "Be not afraid of them that kill the body; and after that have no more that they can do." "Let not your heart be troubled, neither let it be afraid." No pallor on your face. No clammy sweat on your brow. No quiver through your frame.

How may we obtain this lion-heart, which knows no fear in the presence of our foes? There is but one answer possible. Expel fear by fear. Drive out the fear of man by the fear of God. *"Sanctify the Lord God in your hearts."* These words come back to us from a very stormy era in Jewish history. "It was told the house of David, saying, Syria is confederate with Ephraim. And his heart was moved, and the heart of his people, as the trees of the wood are moved with the wind." And the Lord spake to Isaiah his servant, "with a strong hand," saying, Do not join in this panic-stricken cry, or seek to meet confederacy by confederacy; fear ye not their fear, nor be afraid. Sanctify the Lord of hosts Himself; and let Him be your fear, and let Him be your dread. And He shall be for a sanctuary (Isa. 7, 8).

How often we see fear expel fear! The fear of being burnt will nerve a woman to let herself down by a waterpipe from the upper storeys of a house in flames. The fear of losing her young will inspire the timid bird to throw herself before the steps of man, attracting his notice from them to herself. The fear of the whip will expel the horse's dread of the object at which it has taken fright. Oh for that Divine habit of soul which so conceives of the majesty, and power, and love of God, that it dares not sin against Him, but would rather brave a world in arms than bring a shadow over his face! "So did not I," said a sincere and noble man, "because of the fear of God."

And when a man so fears God as that he fears to sin against Him, he will find God to be a sanctuary into which he may retreat, and enjoy an inviolable defence. "Though an host should encamp against me, my heart shall not fear. For in the time of trouble He shall hide me in his pavilion. And now shall mine head be lifted up above mine enemies round about me."

(2) *Be ready always with a reason for your hope.*—We are not always to be talking about our faith, but proving it by divine deeds. But when men, seeing the fruits of our faith, begin to inquire as to its ground and reason, we should always be ready to give them a satisfactory reply.

How remarkable it is, in opposition to many of the contradictory voices of our time, to meet with this clear insistence of the sweet reasonableness of the Christian's hope! The Bible does not appeal to a blind credulity. Many of its statements are above reason ; but none of them are against it. God's continuous appeal is contained in the inspired summons, "Come, let us reason together, saith the Lord." The reasonings of pride will be assuredly puzzled and nonplussed ; but those of meekness will find abundant scope for adoring wonder and assured conviction, in the mighty depths of the thoughts of God.

Young people, the Bible has nothing to fear from the exercise of your reason! It is not possible that the God who built up your brains and endowed you with that marvellous faculty of reason will ever do violence to one of his noblest gifts. Reasoning was a favourite pursuit with the greatest of the Apostles. But reason must ever hold the torch to faith: she must be the handmaid to collect materials for the sanctified judgment ; the analyst to test and separate and re-combine and think over again, as Kepler said, the first thoughts of God. Where reason is the servant of a reverent and holy spirit, as in Newton or Faraday, or the Magi who knelt before the infant Saviour, it is the glory and boast of man. The mistake of so many is not in the exercise of reason, but in putting reason in its wrong place. If you put reason on the throne of your inner life, you may profess to see ; but you will be blind. But if you enthrone faith and hope, whilst reason waits their bidding and obeys their behest, you will be wiser than foe, or teacher, or grey-haired sage (Psa. 119:98—100).

Let us have a reason for our faith, based on personal experience, or observation, or the study of evidence, or of fulfilled prophecy ; or, above all, wrought by the Holy

Spirit in our hearts; and, though we need not be ever obtruding it, let us never flinch from stating it when asked. And let us give our reasons, or conduct our arguments, in a temper which shall be the best evidence of the divine character of our faith. Let there be *meekness* toward the face of man, and *reverential fear* toward the face of God—the temper of those who confess that, at the best, they are but children, gathering a few shells on the shores of the boundless ocean of truth, which sweeps far away to the horizon where eternity and infinity blend.

(3) *Have a good conscience.*—The Apostle Paul also speaks much of conscience, and of the necessity of perpetually exercising ourselves to have a conscience void of offence toward God and man. It is well to obey these repeated commands. The Christian, who faithfully follows the inner voice, and conforms in all things to its behests, will not be far wrong. A "good conscience" implies a "good conversation" in Christ.

There are many kinds of conscience spoken of in Scripture, but this epithet *good* is very comprehensive. Do my readers know what a good conscience is? It is a conscience which is purged from dead works (Heb. 9:14); sprinkled with the blood of Christ (Heb. 10:22), borne witness to by the Holy Ghost (Rom. 9:1): whilst a joy, which is full of glory, wells up within it (2 Cor. 1:12); and as a calm, unruffled lake of peace it reflects the cloudless heaven of God's good pleasure above. Such a conscience is a good companion for our days, and a good bedfellow for our nights. Every effort should be made to preserve its integrity. And when life is moulded by such an inward influence, it will live down all misrepresentation and slander; it will outshine all the mists of envy and malice which have obscured its earliest beams; it will falsify false reports. Detractors shall be ashamed at the triumphant answer made to their accusations by the unblemished beauty of a holy Christian life; whilst those that love God shall take heart. "The righteous shall see it, and rejoice; and all iniquity shall stop her mouth."

Let all who are persecuted possess their souls in patience. Suffering comes to all men; but if we must suffer, it is a thousand times better to suffer for well-doing than for evil-doing, Even here and now it is fraught with blessedness: but who can estimate the exceeding and eternal weight of glory which awaits each member of the noble army of martyrs—from Jesus

Christ, who, before Pontius Pilate, witnessed the good confession, to the least in his kingdom who has stood up for Him unmoved, amid the mockery of school-fellows, or the taunts of a group of shopmates?

19

THE SUBSTITUTIONARY WORK OF CHRIST

"For Christ also hath once suffered for sins, the Just for the unjust, that He might bring us to God."—1 PETER 3:18.

"Christ suffered!" That is the key-note. These believers were suffering—suffering for well-doing. Suffering for conscience' sake. And they were in heaviness through manifold trials. So the Apostle reminds them that Christ also suffered. How sweet is that little word *also!* Cæsar was wont to cheer his troops by addressing them as *fellow*-soldiers. Such is the force of this word. Are you homeless? Christ *also* had not where to lay his head. Are you poor? Christ *also* for our sakes became poor. Are you tempted? Christ *also* hath suffered, being tempted.

But Christ's sufferings are unique! Though He was righteous, He suffered as no other one has for sins; for it is clearly taught here that He suffered as a substitute, "the Just *for* the unjust."

It is quite true, as we are so often told, that the death of the Lord Jesus has had a great moral effect upon men, revealing the love of God, teaching the law of self-sacrifice, showing how keenly sin makes itself felt in the holy sensitive nature of eternal love. But, besides this *subjective* side of our Saviour's death, there is another, an *objective* one. He has not only done something towards men, softening and moving them to thoughts of unselfishness, and deeds of heroism, to which otherwise they must have been for ever strangers; but He has done something also toward the satisfaction of the great laws of the Divine nature, which make for righteousness. And if He had not done the latter, his work in the former had been in vain. It was not enough to touch men, there must be a public reparation made to that violated law, of

117

which both Scripture and conscience speak. So only could penitent sinners be accepted.

It is not necessary that men should understand the philosophy of the Atonement in order to be saved by it. No doubt, thousands have been saved by it who had an erroneous conception of its true significance, in some or even many of its aspects. Certainly our comfort and assurance become stronger in proportion to the clearness and Scripturalness of our views about the death of our Saviour. Still, our salvation does not depend on the accuracy of our intellectual conceptions; but on our trust in the Lord Jesus Christ as a Saviour, who through death and resurrection has acquired the power to save unto the uttermost all that come unto God by Him, their great High Priest.

The substitutionary character of the death of Christ is woven into the texture of Scripture, as the cross into a venerable minster. You cannot eradicate it without destroying the edifice which it underlies. Men must distort the plain meaning of words, ere they can succeed in its elimination from the sacred page.

As we study the Levitical law, we find substitution in every sacrifice. What else is implied in the care to have a stainless victim; in the imposition of hands; in the confession of guilt on the innocent head; in the death of the guiltless, while the guilty goes to his home free? What other truth is taught in the constant reiteration of phrases like that which accosts us in these words—phrases caught from the lips of the Master Himself, who spoke of his life being given *a ransom for many*? What else can explain the marvellous arguments of the Epistles to the Romans and Galatians? If only the masses of Christian people would read the Bible, for themselves, instead of reading so many books about the Bible, they would be compelled to admit that the Scriptures are unanimous in attesting the substitutionary character of the sufferings of Jesus. He died for us. He bore our guilt and shame, our curse and penalty. He took to Himself the penal consequences of human sin, and put them away for ever.

But, in proclaiming this doctrine, let us avoid certain misstatements.

(1) *Let us beware of representing God as loving men only in consequence of Christ's death.*—This is as illogical as it is unscriptural. For it is one of the postulates of all true thinking—that God is; that God is the same; that

118

God is the same Infinite Being, the I AM, the same in the yesterday of the past, and in the to-morrow of the future, as in the to-day of the present. But if the death of Christ be represented as having pacified an inexorable and avenging Deity, causing Him to love those who else must have withered under his relentless hate, it makes Him other than He was and the Divine nature must have suffered a change, which is unthinkable and inadmissible.

The death of Christ is due to the love of God. God gave his Son because He so loved the world. The cross is the expression of a love which is older than the oldest star; more ancient than the most venerable elder who stands in the zenith light of heaven; long as eternity, vast as infinity, deep as the being of God. In this was manifested the love of God, that the Father sent the Son to be the Saviour of the world.

(2) *Let us also beware of making too great a division in the Divine government between God's righteousness and his love.*—There is no collision in God. The nature of God is not defined as righteousness, but as love. If it had been defined as righteousness, it is doubtful if love could have been included. But being defined as love, righteousness is of course included. And there is no collision in God between the two, for his righteousness is a fruit and offspring of his love. He must be righteous, because He is love. He loves; and, therefore, as the Judge of all the earth, He must do right.

It would not be consistent with love if He were to let sin go unnoticed or unpunished; or if He were to allow the moral law to fall into disuse; or if He were to permit us to set at defiance those promptings of our conscience which even we approve. Is it love, which with easy good nature suffers children to do as they like, unrebuked and unrestrained? Is it love to allow murder and lust and rapine to curse a nation of unoffending subjects without an attempt to bring the wrongdoers to justice? Is it love to a man himself to permit him to go on unchecked in a course of ceaseless evil? To ask these questions is to answer them. Love involves Righteousness, and the insistence on the maintenance of right. And in the cross of Jesus there is no variance between the attributes of God. Mercy and truth met together; righteousness and peace kissed each other.

But when men demand that we should refuse to believe in substitution because God is love, and therefore as not requiring an answer to the demands of his

119

justice, we reply that, because He is love, *therefore* He must be just; He must maintain his law; He must exact penalty in respect of the violation of the demands of his righteousness; He must act in the moral sphere as He ever acts in the natural, in allowing law to secure its requisitions and demands when it has been set at nought.

(3) *Let us beware of dissociating the persons of the blessed Trinity in the work of atonement.*—The death of Christ is sometimes so stated as if He stepped in between God and man, and did something on the prompting of his own heart, apart altogether from the Father. And then, of course, the objection arises, Why did God make or permit the innocent One to suffer?

But it must never be forgotten that the death of the cross was the act of the whole Deity. "God was in Christ reconciling the world unto Himself." "Christ, through the eternal Spirit, offered Himself to God." "My Father, which dwelleth in Me, He doeth the works." The Son did nothing of Himself; and how much less could He have wrought his greatest work apart from his Father! He was only translating into human guise and language acts and deeds which He saw his Father do.

And so in the cross we find the eternal God taking to Himself the consequences of human sin; Himself becoming the propitiation for the sin of the world; bearing it Himself; pressed under it as a cart is pressed under sheaves; and putting it away.

This cannot be unjust. It would be unjust to take a good boy and make him suffer for a naughty one; but it cannot be unjust for Bronson Alcott to suffer himself the penalty which should be borne by the boys who have broken the regulations of his school. It cannot be unjust for one to substitute his life for another—else some of the noblest deeds of human history must be expunged.

Yes, reader, you may take this home as yours, and say, thankfully: God has suffered for me in the person of Jesus, the Just for the unjust. You may never have thanked Him, or availed yourself of the benefits of his death, as a man might leave bank-stock to accumulate unclaimed; you may even secure for yourself eternal condemnation by shutting out the love and light of God, and electing to live in the darkness of selfishness and godlessness. And yet it is true that out of his great love the eternal God has done something for you which He

120

never did for angels, and which might make you blessed for ever.

(4) *Let us beware of suggesting that Christ has ceased to suffer.*—There is a sense, of course, in which our Saviour suffered for sins *once*. The direct work of substitution was accomplished on the cross, and was definitely concluded when Jesus cried, "It is finished!" The Resurrection proves that the work of propitiation is an accomplished fact.

But we must not suppose that Jesus has passed into an unsuffering heaven. He still suffers in each of his members. He is crucified afresh when we yield to wilful sins. He travails in birth until his kingdom come. He is touched with the feeling of our infirmities. How can He be at rest, whilst his beloved are tossing in the storm, and the members of his bride are not complete? And through his sufferings blessing is accruing; they cannot be in vain: we shall see all soon; meanwhile let us bear fellowship with Him in his anguish, drinking of his cup, that we may share his glory.

We stand now on the verge of a mysterious and difficult passage; but this much is true and clear, that Christ suffered for us *to bring us to God*. Let us understand that, through faith in Him, we are made one with Him, and stand where He does in the very presence of God, "Made nigh by the blood of the cross." Let us in private prayer, or at the Lord's table, remember that nothing brings us so near as those precious sufferings. And, whenever we feel estranged and distant, let us betake ourselves to the cross; and, sitting there, meditate on those wounds, till we are brought again into rapturous fellowship with our God, our Light, our Love, our exceeding Joy. And then from our sure fellowship with God we may dare to look out on all mysteries, not trying to explain God by the mystery, but the mystery by what we, in our own happy fellowship, know God to be. To whom be glory for ever!

121

20

THE DAYS OF NOAH

*"Put to death in the flesh, but quickened in the spirit,
in which also He went and preached unto the spirits
in prison, which aforetime were disobedient, when the
longsuffering of God waited in the days of Noah, while
the ark was a-preparing, wherein few—that is, eight—
souls were saved through water: which also after a true
likeness doth now save you, even baptism; not the putting away the filth of the flesh, but the interrogation of a
good conscience toward God through the resurrection
of Jesus Christ: who is on the right hand of God, having
gone into heaven; angels and authorities and powers
being made subject unto Him."*—1 PETER 3:18-22 (R.V.).

It would be unwise to load these pages with laboured
references to the various and conflicting interpretations
which have been put upon this difficult and much-de-
bated passage. It appears better, after much studying of
them, to take the words as they stand, and seek to set
forth in clear outline the thought which seems to have
been in the Apostle's mind; so far at least as the present writer conceives of it.

The main idea is of course a comparison between the
experiences of our Lord and those of his suffering followers. The sacred writer was striving to the utmost to
sustain and comfort them under the severe stress of persecution through which they were passing. "Take heart,"
he seems to say, "your sufferings are not exceptional;
they run in the Divine family; even our Master was not
exempt from them: He also suffered in the flesh; but
his sufferings did not stay his blessed ministry; nay, they
even augmented his sphere of usefulness; "He was quickened in spirit," in which also He went forth to herald
his accomplished work in regions to which, but for death,
He had not obtained access. So shall it also be with you.
Your sufferings shall not clip your wings, but add to
your powers of flight. The things which happen to you

shall fall out rather to the furtherance of the Gospel; and it is through death that you must pass up to share his glorious resurrection and imperial power.

I. AN HISTORICAL FACT.—"Put to death in the flesh, but quickened in the spirit, in which also He went and preached unto the spirits in prison, which aforetime were disobedient, when the longsuffering of God waited in the days of Noah."

In one of Isaiah's most splendid passages, the king of Babylon, having fallen at last before that mightier Monarch who comes with equal foot to the hut of the peasant and the palace of the king, is depicted as a thin, pale ghost entering the abodes of the departed. And as he comes, the shades of the kings of the nations and chiefs of the peoples stir themselves, and with thin voices accost him in tones of withering sarcasm: "Art thou also become weak as we? Art thou become like unto us? Is this the man that made the earth to tremble?—that did shake kingdoms?"

But surely the abodes of the departed were stirred after another fashion when the Son of God, having welcomed the dying thief to Paradise, refused to rest there after the strain of his long conflict and agony, but started forth to spend the brief interval until his resurrection in proclaiming with herald voice the wondrous news of accomplished redemption. This is surely the emphatic teaching, not of this passage only, but also of that marvellous announcement of the Apostle Paul in the Epistle to the Ephesians: "He descended into the lower parts of the earth," a phrase which was constantly used among the Jews for the nethermost abyss, the unseen Hadean world, the abode of the departed. On such testimony as this, the Church in all ages has affirmed, *He descended in to Hell* (the word *Hell,* of course, standing, as it does so often on the page of Scripture, for *Hades*). We do not know the full burden of our Master's message there. It is not declared; and all our surmisings must fall short of the reality. All that we need to notice is that the word employed of his ministry is carefully chosen, and only includes the work of a *herald,* as distinguished from that of an *evangelist.*

It may be asked why He preached only to those who were disobedient in the days of Noah? Why were his messages confined to these? Were there not many more who had been disobedient at other periods of the world's sad story? But none of these are excluded. The sacred writer does not say that the Lord addressed no others, but that He certainly addressed these. And our attention is thus focused on *them*, because it was his desire to guide our thoughts to a comparison, already forming in his mind, and casting its shadow over his words, and which would draw lessons from the days of Noah for our own.

Are we then to think that these spirits had another chance, and swarmed, as the mediæval artists loved to depict, in rejoicing crowds after Christ into Paradise? There is nothing of this sort in these words. And it is a mistake to trust to inference in a case so utterly removed from human cognisance and experience. The Bible turns our thought from speculation about the future to life in the living present. "What is that to thee? follow thou Me!"

All that we need to concern ourselves with now is this fragment which Peter has handed down to us from the posthumous sayings of Christ, when He taught them for forty days, and "spoke to them of the things pertaining to the kingdom of God." We must clearly understand that Christ's death did not stop his usefulness, but that He ministered still; just as Joseph, when cut off from his duties in the palace, ministered to his fellow-prisoners, proclaiming to one his deliverance and to another his doom.

II. A CONFESSION.—The story of the Flood seems to have made a great impression on the mind and heart of the Apostle; and the event is constantly on his lips (2 Pet. 2:5; 3:5, 6). And here he follows closely on the words of his Master, who compared the days of Noah with those of the Son of Man.

We need not stay to describe in detail the days which were before the Flood, or *the condition of the old world.* Its course was precisely similar to that of the world around us still. "They ate; they drank; they married, and were given in marriage." The arts and sciences were richly cultivated. Gigantic engineering and architectural works must have abounded, or it would have been impossible to construct such a marvellous vessel as the ark. Refinement and civilisation, side by side with abnormal and horrid crimes. The giddy pursuit of pleasure; the eager search for wealth; the lawless gratification of evil propensity; the reckless disregard of the claims of God; the rush of the torrent of evil and unholiness, in spite of the remonstrances and pleadings of the grey-headed preacher for a hundred years. All these are what we see to-day around us in confused and grievous manifestation.

And there is as little need to describe *the new world* into which Noah and his children stepped down from the mountain slopes on which their ark grounded. How delicious the balmy air, the green grass carpeting the earth, the luxuriant growth of vegetation from the soil enriched and fructified by the alluvial deposit of the waters! It was a world from which sin, and crime, and evil, had been purged, and Creation seemed already to anticipate the vision of the seer "And I saw a new heaven and a new earth ; for the first heaven and the first earth were passed away, and there was no more sea."

But surely that old world is very significant of the old life into which we are born by nature ; and that new world of the new life into which we enter in regeneration. And the Flood of water, through which Noah passed from the old into the new, bearing him onwards on its broad and swelling bosom, from evil and familiar scenes into new and ecstatic surroundings, is a type of the blessed experience of which the Epistles so often speak ; when believers through faith in Jesus pass out of the old life of selfishness and death, into the glorious new life of resurrection blessedness ; when they sit with Christ in the Heavenlies ; when they reckon themselves to be dead indeed unto sin, but alive unto God ; sharing the spirit of the Saviour's death, and of his resurrection : at such times they may be said to repeat the experience of the patriarch, when he passed from the old world into the new.

The early Church was accustomed to set forth this spiritual experience by the outward act of immersion in water. Believers, in confession that they had passed from their previous life of sin into the blessed life of fellowship with the risen Saviour, were buried under water in the likeness of his death, and were lifted again above the water in the likeness of his resurrection. The water in the pool or river might thus be compared to the waters of Noah's Flood, because through each there was a passage from the old to the new, just as in the grave of Jesus there was a passage from the more limited life of the flesh into the freer life of the spirit. "Though we have known Christ after the flesh, yet now henceforth know we Him no more. Therefore if any man be in

Christ he is a new creature: old things are passed away; behold, all things are become new." Baptism, indeed, has no sacramental efficacy; but there are no trifles in the kingdom of God; and obedience to a mere outward rite may make a world of difference between the uneasiness of an evil conscience and the answer of a good one.

III. AN ANALOGY.—We have now seen three facts. First, that Christ's suffering did not hinder his heralding his finished work. Second, that He heralded it to the spirits who in Noah's day were disobedient. Third, that we are like Noah, and Christ, too, in having passed through the waters of death: not the death of the body; but the death of the spirit to its former tastes and delights, because it has entered so fully into the meaning of Christ's death, and into participation with his new life.

What then? Since we have entered into this new and blessed life, are we to be indifferent to those who belong to the old world and life from which we profess to have passed away? Nay, that cannot be; the very metaphors on which we have been dwelling exclude such a thought, and banish it from our serious consideration. In the light of these analogies it cannot be tolerated for a moment.

Of course it would have made the analogy more complete if it could have been said that Noah, after the Flood, had continued preaching to his old companions. But that could not have happened. Yet the same purpose was served, though with a slight change in the person of the herald. For Jesus, whose death and burial were symbolised in the Flood, of whom Noah was a type, and with whose death we are identified, went to these self-same spirits, and spake with them. It was equivalent to Noah going; nay, it was better. Certainly the spirit of Noah's ministry was fully realised in that of his great Antitype.

In my opinion, then, the drift of this passage is to show that it becomes us to herald the tidings of the cross to the old companions of our former life; we are, as it were, to go back to them across the waters of the death flood, not to live again in that world which we have abjured, but to declare the glad tidings of salvation.

Yes, and even their persecution of us should not hinder our efforts for their salvation. Indeed, we shall probably discover that our very sufferings will loose our tongues and enlarge our opportunities. In the stocks we may so sing praise that the prisoners may hear. In Cæsar's house, our bonds for Christ will be manifest in all the palace. In our martyrdoms we shall light fires which shall flame up over the world, and shall never be put out.

Noah's Flood makes us think, not only of that symbolic death which is as much the theme of Rom. 5 as of this passage, but of that literal death, which these believers had to face in the form of martyrdom, and which, unless the Lord come first, we too must experience. But in whatever form death comes to the believer, whether in the acts of daily self-denial, or in the definite abjuring of some form of evil, or in the dissolution of this natural body, it may be met calmly and joyfully, because it is always followed by resurrection.

Through death we follow our Master's steps, which lead to the upland lawns through the valley of the shadow of death. Let us fix our constant gaze on his resurrection, which is a type of ours also, as He takes his place on the right hand of God, "having gone into heaven, angels and authorities and powers being made subject unto Him." We shall share that power only in proportion as we are willing to share his death.

21

ONE WITH HIM IN DEATH

"Forasmuch then as Christ hath suffered for us in the flesh, arm yourselves likewise with the same mind: for he that hath suffered in the flesh hath ceased from sin: that he no longer should live the rest of his time in the flesh to the lusts of men, but to the will of God."—1 PETER 4: 1, 2.

"The rest of his time in the flesh!" Who can tell how long that may be for any one of us? Shorter to some of us than we think; but, in a sense, short to all. The sands run swiftly through life's hour-glass. The shadow hastens to go down upon the dial. The waves eat away so quickly the dwindling shoal of land which crumbles beneath us,

And the years, with inexorable pressure, lay their hands on us, and urge us to flee towards the goal. Such thoughts were much in the Apostle's mind. In the next Epistle, he says, "the putting off of my tabernacle cometh swiftly" (R.V.).

The Christian finds nothing in such thoughts to make him sad. Every milestone marks the growing nearness of his home. The waves cannot be crossed too swiftly by the eager traveller who impatiently counts the hours that interpose between him and the embrace of wife or child. Before us lie the ages of eternity. Hark to the murmur of their waves, as the trained ear catches the beat of the ocean's music, borne on the night breeze! Ages filled with a blessedness of personal enjoyment and rapturous ministry which defy tongue to tell or heart to picture. The dim outlines already sketched stir the heart with ecstasy ; but what will the completed picture be, when God fills in the details with his own hand! Take heart, fellow-sufferers and fellow-workers, our redemption draweth nigh. Day is breaking. "Now is our salvation nearer than when we believed."

But the blessed future must not divert our thoughts from the duties to be discharged during the rest of the time which we are to spend in the flesh. We must not be dreamers, but warriors. We must fill our shortening days with strenuous endeavour ; like the weary toiler who hastens with redoubled energy to finish the garment at which she has been working with sore fingers, because the only candle she can afford is burning low, and must soon flicker out. There is therefore a noise of war in this verse. To arms! to arms! Arm yourselves with the same mind ; and when we ask *What mind?* we are told to arm ourselves with the mind that took Jesus to his death.

In a venerable old church at Innsbruck, famous for containing the tomb of the great Emperor Maximilian, there is a magnificent bronze statue of Godfrey of Boulogne, the illustrious crusader. His head is covered with a helmet, and on the helmet rests a crown of thorns. Of course, there was a meaning in the mind of the artist other than that with which we now invest the strange conjunction. He doubtless designed to represent the sacred cause for which that helmet was donned. But we may discover an apt symbol of the teaching of our Apostle, who unites in these verses the armour of the

Christian soldier, and the recollection of Christ's suffering in the flesh.

This witness of the sufferings of Christ first takes us to the cross; and after gazing reverently on that spectacle of love, we are brought to a point where two ways diverge. And the only way of discovering and maintaining the right path is to imbibe the spirit of that wondrous death; and to glory in the cross of Christ. *In hoc signo vinces*. And thus we shall "no longer live the rest of our time in the flesh, to the lusts of men, but to the will of God."

I.—DIVERGENT PATHS.—(1) On the one side the broad way, trodden by so many feet, of indulgence of the flesh. "The lusts of men." Lust is appetite run wild. There is no harm in any natural appetite, considered in itself, Each is implanted in us for wise and necessary purposes. Man is made as a self-acting machine; and he is not only reminded of necessary duties by the whirr of the alarum, but is driven to perform them by the goad of hungry appetites on the one hand, and by the attraction of satisfied appetites on the other.

But appetite has been spoilt by the Fall. It has become disturbed in its action, so that it does not now work as God intended it to do, when He made man, and pronounced his nature *very good*. When man fell, appetite broke from the enfeebled grasp of the will, and began to seek after its own gratification, irrespective of those necessary uses and legitimate bounds which had been assigned by the Creator's love and wisdom. And so all down the ages, the appetites of man's nature have treated the Imperial will as the barons of the middle ages often treated their Liege Sovereign, whom they practically set at nought, following their own wild and lawless ways. And the mischief of this revolt has been manifested by the way in which the lawlessness of the flesh has infected the mind; so that mind and heart have followed its leadings towards unnatural and excessive indulgence, and men have "fulfilled the desires (or lusts) of the flesh and of the mind."

These habits have descended to us from the generations which have preceded us. Each one of us is therefore born into the world, subject to the action of appetites which are no longer in the same pure and holy state in which they came from the Creator's hand, but are biased strongly in the direction of lawless and unholy manifestation. And if we obey their promptings, as so many do, we become their slaves; sink to the level of the brute creation, which know no law but that of appetite; and come under the wrath of God (Eph. 2:3).

Now, what we need is, not that these appetites should be eradicated—but that they should be controlled; kept only for necessary uses; deprived of all those evil gratifications which have become to them a second nature. Never in this life will they lose the capability of desiring unholy gratification; but those desires, passing as a momentary thrill through our being, and failing to attract or master the will, are not necessarily sins; and it is clearly possible to live in the flesh, which is very sensitive and susceptible to evil suggestion, and yet not to gratify its demands in a single iota beyond the limits of the will and law of God.

This is what the Gospel promises. Not that we should be deprived of any part of our nature. Not that we should never feel the thrill of temptation, and the tendency on the part of our flesh to respond. Not that we should even reach a condition in which it would be impossible to sin. But that the unholy confederacy between the flesh and the spirit should be broken, so that whatever may be the passing spasms of the flesh in the direction of unlawful gratification, they may not be accepted or permitted by the moral nature—the will—the regal individuality of man.

(2) What a glorious contrast to the will of the flesh is "the will of God!" To do this will Jesus came to earth. To do this was, as He said, his "meat." It was the fire-cloud that lit his pathway; the yoke in carrying which He found rest; the Urim and Thummim, which dimmed or shone with heavenly guidance. There is no course more safe or blessed than to live in the will of God. God's will is good will. Where the will of God lies across the wilderness pathway, there flowers bloom, and waters gush from rocks of flint. Sometimes the flesh rebels against it, because it means crucifixion and self-denial: but under the rugged shell the sweetest kernel nestles; and none know the ecstasy of living save those who refuse the broad, easy road of the lusts of men, to climb the steep, upward path of doing the will of God from the heart.

II. THE SECRET AND POWER OF SELF-DENIAL.—It is not easy to refuse that broad, easy road. No effort is required to take it. Life tends to roll easily and luxuriously down its gentle slopes. The stream insensibly bears the boat, gaily decked with flags, and filled with careless or idle pleasure-seekers, toward the fatal rapids. What is the secret which shall lead a man to say "No" to self; to turn a deaf ear to its solicitations; and to face the steep ascent? And, supposing he has the desire to resist, what power is there strong enough to enable him to stem the torrent, beating and seething against him at every stroke?

The answer is found in the cross of our blessed Lord. —"Christ suffered in the flesh." "The pious contemplation of his death will most powerfully kill the love of sin in the soul, and kindle an ardent hatred to it. The believer—looking on Jesus as crucified for him, and wounded for his transgressions; and taking in deep thoughts of his spotless innocency, which deserved no such thing, and of his matchless love, which yet endured it all for him—will then naturally think: Shall I be a friend to that which was his deadly enemy? Shall sin be sweet to me, which was so bitter to Him; and that for my sake? Shall I ever lend it a good look, or entertain a favourable thought of that which shed my Lord's blood? Shall I live in that for which He died, and died to kill in me? Oh, let it not be!"

All this is true; and yet there is a truth beneath. It must never be forgotten that Christ died "in the likeness of sinful flesh." He died, not only for sin, but to condemn sin in the flesh. In his death an entire break was made between the life which He had lived in contact with sin, though Himself sinless, and that other life which He spends on the resurrection side of death. And since we are viewed in the mind and purpose of God, as having died with Him in his death, and being raised in his resurrection, we must also regard ourselves as having passed out of the life in which flesh and sense reign supreme, into that other life where they are for ever left behind, and have no foothold or abode. "In that He died, He died unto sin once; in that He liveth, He liveth unto God. Likewise reckon ye also yourselves to be dead indeed unto sin, but alive unto God through Jesus Christ our Lord."

Let us take high ground in dealing with the solicitations and promptings of the flesh. Let us meet every thrill of passion with the complete indifference, the stony silence, of death. Let us say, as fashionable people are wont to say of acquaintances whom they do not wish to see, *I am not at home to them*.

And so, when strong desires come through our bodies, and strive to send evil thoughts and passions through the heart and will, they will find the fire-proof iron door slammed suddenly in their face, so that the dread contagion may not spread. The flesh may have its desires; but the cleansed heart will refuse to yield to them. And thus the flesh will be crucified and mortified with its affections and lusts, and the conscience kept void of offence.

This power of refusing to harbour or consider the unholy promptings of the flesh is a very blessed one. But it is not of man, nor to be built up by holy resolution or endeavour. It is the power of God in man; the life of the risen Jesus; the grace of the Holy Spirit, who strives against the flesh, so that we may not do the things that otherwise we would (Gal. 5:17, R.V.). Realise that as one with Christ you have, in the mind of God, died. Deliberately choose that death at once and for evermore as your portion and lot. Then look to the Holy Spirit to put the sentence of death into daily and hourly execution. And you will find that, though the flesh still lives, it will no longer govern you; but the Spirit of God will govern it through you, robbing it of power, and keeping it so utterly in subjection that you may be tempted to think that it is changed in nature. This, however, will be a mistake, for if the Spirit's power is relaxed for only an instant, the old fatal habits will re-assert themselves, and if persisted in will work with more than their former force.

III. A STIRRING INJUNCTION.—"Arm yourselves with the same mind." Drink into the spirit of Christ's death till it be repeated in you, and you die to the flesh as He died to it. Thus shall be repeated the ancient legend of the *stigmata*, which grew in the flesh of the saint engaged perpetually in meditating on the wounds of Christ. And every time you dare to refuse the lawless strivings of self, you will enter more into the meaning of his death and of his resurrection. Let us resolutely put this piece of celestial armour on. It will need resolution and determination, as the first shocks of battle will be trying and terrible. But victory is sure. And though there will be no cessation in the temptation, there will be cessation in the yielding to it, which is sin: "For he that hath died is freed from sin" (Rom. 6:7). And in time the bodily

132

desires, long thwarted, will give less and less trouble, as if they were weary of the incessant defeat.

"Wouldst thou then have much power against sin, and much increase of holiness, let thine eye be much on Christ ; set thine heart on Him ; let it dwell in Him, and be still with Him. When sin is likely to prevail, go to Him, tell Him of the insurrection of his enemies, and thy inability to resist, and desire Him to suppress them, that they may gain nothing by their stirring but some new wound. If thy heart begin to move towards sin, lay it before Him: the beams of his love shall eat out that fire of those sinful lusts. Wouldst thou have thy pride, and passions, and love of the world killed, go sue for the virtue of his death, and that shall do it. Seek his spirit the spirit of meekness, humility, and Divine love. Look on Him, and He shall draw thy heart heavenwards, and unite it to Himself, and make it like Himself. And is not that the thing thou desirest?"

22

THE BREATH OF ETERNITY

"For the time past of our life may suffice us to have wrought the will of the Gentiles, when we walked in lasciviousness, lusts, excess of wine, revelling, banquetings, and abominable idolatries: wherein they think it strange that ye run not with them to the same excess of riot, speaking evil of you: who shall give account to Him that is ready to judge the quick and the dead. For this cause was the gospel preached also to them that are dead, that they might be judged according to men in the flesh, but live according to God in the spirit. But the end of all things is at hand: be ye therefore sober, and watch unto prayer."—1 PETER 4:3-7.

There is a great contrast between the believers of the Apostolic age and ourselves. And this contrast is shown, not so much in the truths held and believed, or in devotion towards the Lord Jesus, as in the different attitude taken up and maintained towards the great future.

133

With them eternity had already begun. It dated from the moment in which they received Christ into their hearts. The fact of their being in the body did not obscure their perception of the union subsisting between them and their risen Lord, so close and intimate that where He was *there* they also were. His death had cut them also off from the world which had crucified Him. His grave lay as an impassable barrier between them and the course of human society, which had refused and rejected Him. In his resurrection and ascension they had participated. Where their treasure was, there their hearts were also. In Him they had already become denizens and citizens of the world where He was King, sitting in the Heavenlies. True, they had their dwelling in the world to do their necessary business according to the will of God, to learn lessons that could only be learnt under the conditions of our present mortal life, and to act as an antiseptic to the evil around. But this was compatible with their dwelling in spirit in their true home and rest, confessing that they were strangers and pilgrims on the earth.

The voyager detects the near proximity of land by the fresh land-breeze which breathes in his face, wafting the sounds and scents of forest, or prairie, or heather-covered hill. So, through these Epistles, we inhale another atmosphere than that with which we are so familiar in modern Christian societies. We live in the world and pay occasional visits into the unseen and eternal; those early Christians lived in the unseen and eternal, and paid periodic necessary visits into the world. We conform to the world; *they* were transformed by the daily renewing of their minds. We read the society papers, discuss society gossip, send our children into society, and strive to hold our own in dress and appointments with the cream of society around us; *they*, on the other hand, were thought strange and ridiculous, because they lived amongst men as "the children of the resurrection." Surely the contrast is not to our credit, although we vaunt our fancied superiority.

There are many symptoms of this state of mind in the passage before us. The limited time or duration of our life as contrasted with the infinite stretch of future existence; the reference to Him who is ready to judge, as if the great white throne were already erected in mid-heaven, and men were being arraigned before it, preparatory to the solemn session of the Judge; the piercing cry as of the last herald angel, that the end of all things is at hand—all these indicate the mood of the Apostle's soul. He stood in the light of eternity. Its breath was upon his face. Its spirit was in his heart. And it was under the deep impression of these momentous realities that he exhorted those whom he addressed, as pilgrims and strangers, to abstain from fleshly lusts. And what stronger motive could he have employed?

I. A BLACK ENUMERATION.—"Lasciviousness, lusts, excess of wine, revellings, banquetings, and abominable idolatries." It is a dark picture, reminding us of 1 Cor. 6:9-11. But it is a faithful delineation of the state of the world, in spite of the loftiest teachings of philosophy and morals. Ordinary readers can form but a very inadequate conception of the gross evils before which the ancient world was simply rotting away at the time of the Advent. The extent of the evil is veiled by the dead languages which contain the record for all time. Suffice it to say that the dialogues of Plato, containing some of the noblest speculations of heathendom, are disgraced by the unblushing discussion and approval of sins which are condemned by the police-courts of every nation in Christendom. There is, therefore, abundant corroboration of this inspired picture of the state of the society of that day. And perhaps its very vileness had a salutary effect upon the Christians of that age, in compelling them to come out and be separate. The curse of our time is that Satan has counterfeited so much of Christianity, and has sought to hide a Godless civilisation under the veneer of Christian terms.

We need not dwell on the various evils enumerated, except to note how closely excess of wine is connected with abominable idolatries; and to ask whether any use of wine is not excessive, unless it be taken for some very distinct purpose of health, prescribed by medical authority—and, even then, often mistakenly. We desire rather to call attention to the strong phraseology employed to describe these sins, when the Apostle calls them, as the Greek word indicates, "stagnant pools of havoc-making sin."

Men are tormented by thirst. That thirst was meant to bring them to the river of water of life, which flows from the throne of God. But as they refuse to follow it thither, they are given up to follow it to the brackish stagnant pools of the desert, at which the very beasts

135

would refuse to drink. The music-hall, the gambling den, the casino, the public-house, the abode of shame, are so many fœtid pools, at which men seek to quench a thirst which can be slaked with nothing short of the living God. Oh, when will they learn their fatal error! How shall they be warned! Can we not get one draught of throne-water into their tortured throats, to give them an abhorrence of all other beverage beside! "Ho, every one that thirsteth, come ye to the waters."

And as to havoc! What a tale is being told by every newspaper of the havoc being wrought in the votaries of sin. Havoc in estate, fortune, health, happiness, reputation, and usefulness. Wretched bodies, beneath whose weight of corruption the spirit seems almost to have expired. Wretched lives, like the frigate which so gaily leaves the harbour to-day, but is torn by the jagged fang of the rock to-morrow, and goes down in deep water. Wretched souls, without God, or hope, or love, or any trace of their high origin and Divine equipment. Well may the Lamb of God still wear the guise of the Sufferer, in the midst of the throne of God, while sin still works such havoc among a race which He loves more than Himself.

Men of the world think it strange that we do not run with them to the same excess of riot. They know what we renounce, but not what we receive. They see us flinging away the rank water from the stinking bottle-skins, but they do not see us drinking down long draughts of everlasting life. They cannot understand that what we have in Christ makes all things else taste insipid and forbidding. If they only knew, they would see that THEY are acting strangely, and not we. For, as we see what they miss, and how hard their service is, and how many bitters mingle with their sweets, we often think it strange that they prefer husks to bread, paste diamonds to jewels, and Marah to Elim.

Any time spent in the lusts of the flesh is too long. The time past may well suffice. Oh the bitter regrets which the memory of past sins breeds in the saved soul! What would it not give to be able to obliterate the record, and to look back on an unsullied page! But this may not be. Our only comfort is that He who says that the time for watching is over, also says that there is yet opportunity to retrieve the past, and promise to restore the years which the cankerworm and caterpillar have eaten.

II. AN ARRESTING CONSIDERATION.—"Who shall give account to Him that is ready to judge the quick (*i.e.,* the living) and the dead." It is related of Latimer that, when summoned to take his last trial before vindictive foes, he was somewhat loose and careless in his replies, till, in a pause, he caught the sound of a pen behind the arras, transcribing every word he spoke; and immediately he began to weigh his words with minute and exacting care. Thus we are urged to withdraw ourselves from the ways of those who speak evil of us and blaspheme God, and to live soberly, righteously, and godly, in this present evil world, because the Judge standeth at the door.

There is a sense, in which, of course, the judgment awaits men on the other side of death—the judgment seat of Christ for his servants, to adjust their rewards, and the final judgment for the unsaved and ungodly, into which we who are one with Him can never come; but it is also true that we are now in the presence of our Judge. He is ready; He is at the door. The time is come that judgment must begin; and it begins at the house of God.

"Soldiers," said Napoleon to his army, as it passed under the shadow of the pyramids, "forty centuries look down upon you." But if there be an inspiration to valour in the thought of the venerable past, surely there must be a stimulus to holy living in the thought that all our life is naked and open to the eyes of Him with whom we have to do, whose decisions are even now beginning to register themselves in our history.

From the living the Apostle turns to the dead, to those who had died lately as sufferers and martyrs in the persecutions, which were already beginning to thin the ranks of the Church. He grants, without hesitation, that they had been adjudged to suffer as much as human nature could, and as if they had been the greatest sinners among their fellows. But after all, it was only "according to men," and "in the flesh"; and from their sufferings he passes to their great reward, and sums it up in saying, they "live according to God in the spirit." Against the agonies and tears and adverse judgment of their age, through which the martyr host was called to pass, we must ever set the glories of their reward, as they live in the front ranks of the redeemed, and sun themselves in the light of God's face. And if we are called to share their fate "according to the flesh," let us cheer our hearts by remembering that we shall also share their life "according to God in the spirit," in that world where human judgments are passed under the scrutiny of eternity, and human verdicts are liable to be reversed with no option of appeal.

How tender the thought of eternity makes us of other men! Would that it were graven on our hearts, as on the pavement before Robert Annan's door, that we might bear their rebuffs, and testify against their sins, as those who are already treading the streets of the Holy City, and are carrying in their hearts the music of the everlasting song

III. A CLARION CALL.—"The end of all things is at hand: be ye therefore sober, and watch unto prayer." The end of the Jewish State was impending. The throes of dissolution were already being felt. Soon the venerated system in the heart of which the Church had been nurtured was to split, as the shell of the acorn bursts before the opening of life.

The end of the age of prophets and kings; of a material city of God; of the rites and ceremonies of a typical religion—had come. There was anguish and foreboding in pious hearts as they saw the destruction of a system in which they had been wont to shelter. The birds are scared when they see the tree where many generations have had their nests, swaying to its fall beneath the woodman's axe. The air is full of dust and pother as the scaffolding is taken down, which has come by long usage to be considered part of the true temple, though in reality it obscures its proportions and beauty. But the Apostles were able to look on without dismay, knowing that the things which were being shaken and removed were only the things which were made, and that they were being put out of the way of those things which cannot be shaken and shall remain.

The time in which we are living is remarkably similar. This also is the end of the age. "The old order changeth, giving place to new." God is beginning to wrap it together as a worn-out vesture. Institutions, expressions, long-cherished methods—are being put into the crucible; with the sure result that only the transient and material shall be dissolved, and there shall emerge the new heavens and earth in which dwelleth righteousness.

Our duty in this crisis is twofold: (1) *Be sober.*—Let there be a noble self-restraint in respect to even lawful appetite, and in the use of all the acquisitions and possessions of life. Let the flowing habits, the vestments of the soul, be girt up around the loins. Let there be no entanglement on the part of Christ's soldiers in the affairs of this life, that we may please Him who has chosen us to be his soldiers, and that we may be ready to be up and away whenever the trumpet shall ring out the summons for the exodus, or the voice shall be heard proclaiming the Bridegroom's advent.

(2) *Watch unto prayer.*—The Lord depicts the faithful servant on the watch for his master's coming, though the long hours of the night have begun to yield to the summons of the dawn, and all around him his fellow-servants are wrapped in slumber.

> *"Oh, happy servant he*
> *In such a posture found!"*

Be that posture ours, standing at the oriel window which looks out towards the eastern sky, filling the hours with prayer for his speedy advent, so that before ever He comes and knocks, we may be down to greet Him on the doorstep, and receive his salutation of peace, his word of "Well done!"

23

LOVE COVERING SINS

"Above all things, being fervent in your love among yourselves: for love covereth a multitude of sins."—1 PETER 4:8 (R.V.)

It need not surprise us to find the Apostle Peter insisting so strenuously on love. At a never-to-be-forgotten interview, the Master thrice reminded him that the supreme qualification for ministry was love. And now he takes care to insist upon the possession of the gifts with which they have been entrusted.

Above all things.—It were better to dispense with all else in the Christian's character and work than to miss love; though, in point of fact, where this is in operation, all that is likely to impress and touch men must be present also. This love must, of course, go forth in its sympathies and activities to all the world; but it should begin at home. We must have love *among ourselves* as believers in the same Lord, before we can presume to speak of our love to the great world of men around. Nor must it be a Platonic love, a love of the cold light of reason; it must be *fervent,* at boiling point, on full stretch, going to the furthest extents of love, and in doing so, learning the breadths and lengths of the unsearchable love of God.

But we have now rather to consider the way in which this love will act; for it is remarkably practical. The state of heart which weeps tender tears and expresses itself in rhapsody or sentiment, but at the same time does nothing to relieve distress or to sacrifice itself for others, is the shadowy ghost of love, its imitation and counterfeit. Love gives itself; pours itself forth as a libation; counts all things loss in comparison with the benefit of the one on whom it has centred itself. It imperils its life to fetch water from the well of Bethlehem; breaks alabaster boxes of very precious ointment on the person of its beloved; and braves the reproaches of a world in arms—surprised to find any one considering the pain or hardship great. Oh for love like this!

I. LOVE COVERS A MULTITUDE OF SINS (8).—These sins are, of course, not those of the man who loves, but the sins of those with whom he is brought in contact. The thought is, in fact, quoted from Proverbs 10:12. And the whole conception may have been based on the filial act of Noah's sons, of whom it is recorded that they took a garment, and laid it upon both their shoulders, and went backward, and covered their father's drunken sin.

How few men there are without grave faults! "Even in the most highly cultivated countries there are tracts of land which have never been brought under the plough; so it is with the characters of some men—perhaps of most men; there are patches of waste ground lying here and there utterly useless, offensive to the eye, and covered, not with wholesome corn, but with briars and nettles and weeds of poisonous quality." We need not now enter into the question of how these faults come to be permitted by devout and saintly souls; but, if it be so with respect to these, how much more must it be the case in respect to those who do not avow allegiance to the holy Gospel.

Men are constantly sinning against one another. They take unfair advantage; they deceive with lying words; they lose their temper to each other's face, and slander behind each other's back; they grasp at their own pleasure or gain, irrespective of what it may cost to those whom they were bound to consider; they snarl, and bite, and devour, as the wild beasts of the forest. Ah, what wrongs man has endured at the hands of his fellow!

There are some imperfections in men which, though not to be classed in the front rank of sins, are yet very trying and hard to bear. The vanity which is so self-conscious, and is always expecting flattery or extorting it. The discontent which is ever repining. The restlessness which betrays the irritable brain and the overstrained nervous system. The petulance of the sufferer; and the growing penuriousness of the aged. The cynical temper of those who feel that they have not received their dues in life, and depreciate others. The recklessness which is courage exaggerated. All these are irksome and fretting, and produce almost as much revulsion as blacker kinds of sin.

Now we are not required to form a false judgment of these people, and to think or say that they are not offenders. If they are doing wrong, it is not our duty to whitewash their fault and to call evil good. There is rather a temptation to do so; because, if we are not too strict with others, we can venture to be lenient to ourselves. Thus our moral sense will become warped and deteriorated. To gloss over the faults of other men is often the first step to making light of our own. We must be very careful, therefore, not to look at these faults with that easy good-nature which is careless of the distinction between white and black.

And, again, we are not required to abjure all words of reproach or methods of punishment.—There is a soft, weak, reckless kind of feeling abroad in society, which is always saying pretty nothings, and sprinkling rose water on open sewers, but which does not dare to be stern and severe, and true to righteousness. This is not Christian love; though it is often mistaken for it. The love which God inspires will withhold; will leave the results of sins to work themselves out in the life; will dare to linger for three days at a distance, rather than go at once in answer to the appeal for aid. There is nothing so wholesome, so salutary, so strong—as Christian love.

But with all these limitations, love does cover a multitude of sins.

(1) *It forgives.*—This is a marvellous prerogative placed within our reach, in the exercise of which we are most like God. Certainly in this world only shall we have opportunity to put it into exercise. When once we have entered the world where there is no sin, then will the need of mercy stay ; other graces finding full development. The Christian heart does not wait for confession or explanation, but so soon as it is sensible of having been wronged, it looks to heaven asking the Father to forgive ; and it cherishes the sweet sense of forgiveness, until it has an opportunity of pronouncing its absolution to the contrite offender. We are to be imitators of God in the swiftness and completeness of his forgiveness.

(2) *It avoids giving occasion for sin.*—It has been said that if you have a favourite horse, which always takes fright and shies at a certain point in the road, you are careful to pass along another road, if possible ; or, by speaking to him kindly, to coax him to go by without fear. So if you are aware that a certain subject will always invoke an outburst of hot temper in your friend, true love will lead you to avoid it. You will not needlessly incite to sin if you know how to avoid giving the first inducement.

(3) *It is quick to discern some generous construction to put upon the fault, or to quote some consideration to weigh in the opposite scale.*—"True, he was excessively dull and slow ; but then how trustworthy and reliable!" "Yes, he was very irritable and abrupt ; but then, remember what a strain he has been under lately in his business, not leaving the factory or counting-house till late at night, and going back early in the morning, with no recreation or respite." "Granted, that he is now becoming soured and crabbed ; but, then, what a glorious man he was in those earlier days, when he stood in the breach!" "Are you sure that there is not some other explanation possible for his action?" In some such ways as these, Christian love argues with itself and others ; and, as the result, many a sin is hindered on its way.

(4) *It rebukes with great tenderness.*—There are cases where duty demands public censure. The sore must not lie covered up, lest it prove to be deadly. It must be lanced or it cannot be cured. But the lancing is done

with exquisite tenderness. The wrong-doer is reproved, rebuked, and exhorted, but with all long-suffering (2 Tim. 4:2). The man overtaken with a fault is restored in the spirit of meekness (Gal. 6:1).

"There is a great deal of spiritual art and skill required for dealing with another's sins; it requires much spirituality of mind, much prudence, and a mind clear from passion, for that blinds the eye and makes the hand rough, so that a man neither rightly sees nor rightly handles the sore he goes about to cure; and many are lost through the ignorance and neglect of that due temper which should be brought to this work." But love gives the delicacy and tact required.

II. LOVE AFFORDS UNGRUDGING HOSPITALITY (9).—This does not mean the giving of extravagant feasts, but rather the calling in of the poor, the lame, the halt, and the blind, who cannot recompense. It is right to look on the home as a talent for God's service, and to use its guest-chamber, not only for our friends, but for his servants. Those who live at the sea-side, or in salubrious neighbourhoods, should consider whether they cannot refresh and re-invigorate some jaded worker. And those who live in large towns might throw open their rooms to young people fresh from the country, and sorely tempted to go wrong for want of a friendly welcome into a circle like that left far away. "Be not forgetful to entertain strangers." In the person of his children the Master still often asks the question, "Where is the guest-chamber?"

Without grudging.—To God the intention of the heart is all important. He loveth a cheerful giver. He takes such delight in doing good that He has no sympathy with anything like reluctance. Not that hospitality should necessarily be profuse: for, if it be, it is difficult to maintain; besides reminding the guest that he is regarded as a stranger: only that which is done should be done freely, gladly, with the whole heart. There is no hospitality so grateful as that which makes the stranger feel at home, because there is nothing forced or restrained, and he is permitted to feel completely at his ease.

III. LOVE MINISTERS (10. 11).—The Apostle speaks here, not so much of the extraordinary gifts with which the early Church was endowed, but of those which are possessed by us to-day. The gifts of speech, of wealth, of administrative ability, of song. All these things are *gifts* from the hand of God. There is nothing to be proud of ; for we have nothing that we have not received. And instead of envying another, let us thank God for what he also has received, asking that we may benefit by it, and win as much of its grace as possible.

Each member of the Church is a steward, entrusted with something.—No note without significance. No wheel without its function. No pin or axle without importance. "Each man hath received a gift." Oh, you who are doing nothing to make the world better, it is not for want of a talent, but because you are not using the talent which you have. You have buried it somewhere in a napkin. Go and unearth it, and put it out to usury. It may not be brilliant ; but, so surely as it has been given, you will be held accountable for its use. The ability to give is a great talent, and is as much a sacred trust as the power to teach or preach. Let us never forget that we are not owners, but stewards who must render an account of our stewardship to the Master ; and He may even now be at the door. It matters not what our fellow-servants think or say, so long as we are right with Him, and are developing and administering to our utmost the precious talents with which we are endowed. The main object with each of us should be, to act up to the ability which God hath given.

Manifold grace is many-coloured grace. As when a ray of light breaks into a spray of many hues, so each of us receives God's grace at a different angle, and flashes it back broken up into some fresh colours. In some it is speech ; in others service ; in others giving. But all are called to bear their several parts in the great household of the Church, the management of which may be thoroughly disorganised by the sloth or refusal of one.

In all the motive should be the same. The service may be great or small, conspicuous or obscure ; but the glory of God must be the supreme passion. If we work from any other motive, we are doomed to disappointment. But none can work for this in vain. In our failure and death, if He wills it, He can be glorified. Let us bring Him glory through Jesus Christ, our Mediator and Priest ; and may it flow in towards Him from us, and from all created beings for ever and ever. Amen.

24

THE MOTIVE OF OUR LIVES

"If any man speak, let him speak as the oracles of God; if any man minister, let him do it as of the ability which God giveth: that God in all things may be glorified through Jesus Christ, to whom be praise and dominion for ever and ever."—1 PETER 4:11.

Before passing on to consider the fiery trial which is to try us, it seems wise to stay very briefly to consider the master-motive which should inspire our lives—namely, "that God in all things may be glorified."

This was the motive which actuated our blessed Lord. —When He took upon Himself the form of a servant, and was made in the likeness of men, He set before Him, as the ideal and purpose of his life, to glorify his Father. He speaks of Himself as seeking not his own glory, but the glory of Him that sent Him (John 7:18). On the review of his life from the vantage ground of death He rejoiced that He glorified his Father on the earth, and had finished the work given Him to do (John 17:4). He asked for glory only as the condition of glorifying his Father the more (1). And He promised to answer prayer, with the avowed intention that God the Father should be glorified in the Son (John 14:13).

We learn from the Lord's own words that the Spirit would glorify Him, after He had passed away to the Father; and what the Spirit does for the Son, through the ages, that the Son also does, and did, for the Father. So that from the perpetual ministry of the Spirit we may form some conception of the ministry of the Son, during his earthly life, and throughout that blessed life which He is spending within the vail, intense, earnest, and blessed; and which is inspired by the same passion for his Father's glory as animated Him in the days of his flesh (John 17:4, 5).

But what is glory, and how can God be glorified? Glory is the manifestation of the hidden attributes of the ever-blessed God. He dwells in light which is so transcendent in its burning purity that no mortal eye could bear the blaze which enwraps his Being. But, if unknown, He would be for ever unappreciated and unloved. How could men or angels worship an inaccessible and unknown God? But Jesus Christ, who has dwelt for ever in the bosom of the Father, has declared Him: has brought out his attributes from their dark obscurity, and has displayed them. He has been the organ through which the Divine nature has manifested itself; and as it has been manifested, God has been known and loved and adored by countless myriads who have seen his glory in the face of Jesus Christ, and have fallen down in ecstasies of devotion, ascribing glory to Him that sitteth on the throne, and to the Lamb.

The prism, which shows the exquisite tints that hide in sunbeams, glorifies the sun and its Maker. The artist who reads nature's secrets, and catches bewitching smiles which are only seen by her lovers, glorifies Him who lives behind all nature. The student who shows some unsuspected beauty in our favourite author, adds to that author's glory in our esteem. So, though in an infinitely superior sense, as the Son has been the medium through which the Father has shone forth, and has attracted the admiration and homage of all intelligent creatures, we may rightly say that in Him He has been glorified.

This was so in creation, when the creative qualities of the Almighty passed through the Son into efflorescent beauty. It has been so in providence, wherein the sustaining grace of God has been revealing itself through successive ages of activity. It was especially so in the life and words and death of the Redeemer. These were windows into the heart of God. Never had He been known unless in contact with human sin, His Being had broken into the prismatic band of colour which makes the Gospels the priceless possession of mankind. And possibly in those events which are yet to happen, we shall see how the Lord Jesus will contrive at every turn to bring into ever clearer prominence attributes of the Divine Being, of which we know little or nothing, or which only glimmer on our sight, like some distant star on the very confines of creation.

This was equally the motive of the Apostles.—Not for emolument, or human praise; not for power or love of place; not for the souls of men only; but for the glory of God, did they reckon not their lives dear, but endured

146

hardships and persecutions even to martyrdom itself. They yearned to show men how good and glorious He was; or to open the cavern of some heart to receive into its depths his light—that so the extent of his empire might be increased by one more being brought from darkness into light, and from the power of Satan unto God.

And this should be our motive.

(1) *It would never disappoint.*—If we work for any lower motive, we are always liable to disappointment. Either the desire of our hearts is not realised, or, when we have attained it, we are oppressed with a vague sense of dissatisfaction and depression. But here is a motive which can never mislead us. It is always in front of us. It is an ever-fresh inspiration, ennobling, and inspiring, and elevating. When we have done our best, it is still in front of us, beckoning us to loftier ascents, to more strenuous endeavours. And the impression produced on us is one of adoration and devotion, which make all our life and work a means of grace.

If we are sensible of working from a wrong or inferior motive, let us bring our being to God, and tell Him that we desire and will nothing so eagerly as to live and work from this loftiest of motives. Ask Him to create the clean heart, and to renew the right spirit. Expect that by his Spirit He will replace the worse by the better, till your soul is on fire for the glory of God.

Many need this word. They are working for the salvation of others; to increase their congregation; to stop the ravages of sin; or to alleviate the distress of those immediately dependent on some sad case of dissolute and shameful behaviour. We cannot wonder at these motives: but they are not the best; and their presence will go far to explain the failure under which many devoted workers groan. Whether you work for God, or pray for the coming of the Spirit, or engage in philanthropic enterprise, be sure to do all for the glory of God.

(2) *It will dignify all life.*—We make distinctions which do not hold beyond the low ceiling of this world. We speak of some things as sacred and some as secular; of great and little; of religious and the reverse. We judge things by their appearances and the space they take among men. We forget that with God the difference is entirely one of motives. A sacred motive makes everything sacred; a secular one drags down the most holy office to its own Godless level. Little things become great when wrought

from a great motive of love and consecration; but a mean motive will make the gift of a millionaire shrink into a nutshell as small as itself. A religious man will tie everything with a double knot of faith and prayer to God; an irreligious man makes the table of the Lord to become a table of demons.

Men often chafe at being confined to the secularities of daily life, and long to be set free to follow the work of the minister or missionary. If any such read these lines, let them ask their hearts if they are entirely yielded up to the Lord Jesus. If so, let them understand that He has put them where they are for a specific purpose. And then let them fill that position for Him and in his strength, so that many a gleam of his loveliness may be emitted through their behaviour; and men may think better of Him for their sake. "To me to live is Christ"; that Christ may be magnified. Whatever our daily occupation, we should engage in it for the same high motive which should animate the chosen Apostle, or the burning seraph; inscribing on the threshold of each new day, "Glory to God in the highest." "Whether therefore ye eat or drink, or whatsoever ye do, do all to the glory of God" (1 Cor. 10:31).

But, after all, let it never be forgotten that no motive, however pure and lofty, can make our service perfectly acceptable to God. No glory can accrue to Him save through the merit of the Lord Jesus. And, therefore, the Apostle takes care to add, "glorified through Jesus Christ" (11). There is only one way to God; and our incense must be scattered on coals taken from the true altar, or it can never rise up acceptable and pleasing to Him.

Oh to be animated with absorbing desires for the glory of God! For this to live, and, if need be, die! For this to do the tiniest acts of self-sacrifice and service; and to forget hardship and difficulty in the all-absorbing passion! Let this be our life-motive. Not content to wait for distant ages, let us now ascribe to Him "praise and dominion." Let our lips be full of his praise, and our lives obey his dominion, and let there arise from each moment of our poor lives the glad, and heartfelt, and devout Amen.

25

NOT SO STRANGE

"Beloved. think it not strange concerning the fiery trial which is to try you, as though some strange thing happened unto you: but rejoice, inasmuch as ye are partakers of Christ's sufferings ; that, when his glory shall be revealed, ye may be glad also with exceeding joy. If ye be reproached for the name of Christ, happy are ye ; for the spirit of glory and of God resteth upon you: on their part He is evil spoken of, but on your part He is glorified."—1 PETER 4: 12-14.

Once it seemed strange to the Apostle Peter that his Master should think of suffering. Now he thinks it strange that He could have imagined anything else ; and he writes to the scattered Christians, bidding them not to count it strange if their path lies through fiery trial and bitter pain.

"Think it not strange!" But it does seem strange— strange that the waters of a full cup should be wrung out to the saints, whilst sinners walk on the sunny side of the hedge! Strange that the wicked should be permitted to plot so much and so successfully against the righteous! Strange that the profane sit on the judgment seats at which the godly and devoted are arraigned for no other fault than their endeavours for the good of men! Strange to find some of the sweetest and noblest of God's children racked with agony, dying of cancer, beset with poverty, misunderstanding, and hatred.

To the eye of natural reason it was strange that thousands of martyrs should die in the amphitheatres of Rome, and illumine the public gardens, whilst Nero revelled in his splendid palace-halls! Strange that the saints of the Lord should suffer in dungeon and at stake, whilst a Bonner, a Jeffries, a Claverhouse. gained place and pelf by their destruction! Strange that the progress of the Church has always been marked by the thin trail of blood! It is hard not to think it strange. And yet it would be stranger still if it were not so. Let us now look into THE CONSIDERATIONS WHICH ROB SUFFERING OF ITS STRANGENESS:

(1) *This world is in revolt.*—Marvellous to relate, it has, like ancient Israel, rejected God from its throne, and has chosen another god, who is repeatedly referred to by our Lord as "the prince of this world." Saul rules the visible world; while David, the rightful king, is keeping himself hid amid the growing numbers of those who love him. Is it to be wondered at that the servants of the Divinely designated Prince should experience rough treatment at the hands of the rebel forces who disown his sway? It could not be otherwise.

(2) *Along this way the Master went.*—From the moment of his birth, when Herod sought to slay Him, to the last moment of his life, He was a lily among thorns, a silent lamb among strangers. His brethren hated Him, and could not speak peaceably to Him. Those whom He came to gather, as a hen gathers her chickens under her wing, refused Him with contumely and reproach, and finally wounded Him to the death. There never was such a union in hatred as that which encircled Jesus as with a ring of forked flame, when He went to the cross. Ah, blessed One, Prince in the realm of misery, as in all other spheres, Thou hast endured the contradiction of sinners against Thyself, and it is not for us to choose a happier pathway, or an easier lot, lest we should seem not to belong to Thee or to bear Thy name.

(3) *This is the way home.*— When Samuel bade adieu to the young king-elect, on whose life the eyes of all Israel were about to turn, he told him of certain signs which should befall him on his way (1 Sam. 10.). And the prophet probably did this to give him materials for forming a true estimate of the Divine authority of the communication which he had just received. He must have felt more and more convinced at every step that Samuel was a true prophet, and that he was on his pre-destined way. So when we see or experience the hate entertained towards Christianity and Christians by those whom they mean to benefit, and realise that it exactly fulfils the repeated predictions of our blessed Lord, we, too, are persuaded that we are on

> "the way the prophets went,
> The road that leads from banishment."

If we were universally beloved, and no voice were ever raised in hatred or calumny, we might truly question whether we were at all on the heavenward track. It is stated so emphatically that if we are without chastisement, whereof all are partakers, then we are bastards and not sons. And, again, it is said, through much tribulation we must enter into the kingdom of God.

It must be so just in proportion to the sincerity and consistency of our religious life. If we are living as we should, we condemn the world around us. "There is in the life of the Christian a convincing light which shows the deformity of the works of darkness, and a piercing heat which scorches the ungodly and troubles their consciences. This they cannot endure, and hence rises in them a contrary fire of wicked hatred, and out of this the fiery trials of the godly."

(4) *There is an object in such suffering.*—Though it may seem to spring causeless from the ground, yet in point of fact it is carefully designed by the skill of the great Artificer. There may have been many a previous secret prayer for growth in grace and usefulness; and the answer has come in the use of fire, file, and hammer, wielded by God, though furnished by the hatred of the sons of men. The malignant deed of cruelty may proceed from the treachery of a Judas; but the cup must be taken as from the Father's hand. Though the missile may be hurled by malice and illwill, yet if it is permitted to pass through the environing presence of God, it has become his appointment for the refining and maturing of the sufferer's character. In this sense his permissions become his appointments. We cannot become new sharp threshing instruments, without fire; and therefore it is not strange when we are plied by it to the uttermost. But One sits beside who holds our pulse between his fingers, and will not let the heat be too searching, or the discipline too severe. There is no other way of eliminating much of the selfish dross of our natures.

(5) *Herein we partake of Christ's sufferings.*—Of course there is a sense in which Christ's sufferings are unapproachable. They stand as a solitary obelisk on the sands of time. He trod the winepress *alone*. There is no sorrow like unto his sorrow, in the day in which the Lord afflicted Him. And yet there is a sense in which we fill up that which is behind of the sufferings of Christ. His life in us meets the same treatment as it did in Him. Knowing that we cannot partake of his sacrificial and substitution-

ary sufferings, yet we may all know something of his other sufferings when He was tempted; when He fore-saw the doom of men, and wept; when He endured the contradiction of sinners against Himself; when He sur-rendered Himself to do and suffer the holy will of God! Ah, it is good to share anything with Him. Sweet things are bitter when He is absent, and bitter things sweet if He is near. Would that we were closer drawn into his most intimate friendship, though the connecting links were clamps of iron, forged in the fiery furnace!

As St. Bernard said, He always fled when they wanted to make Him King, and presented Himself when they wanted to crucify Him. With this clearly in mind let us not hesitate to adopt the noble words of Ittai the Gittite: "As the Lord liveth, and as my lord the king liveth, surely in what place my lord the king shall be, whether in death or life, even there also will thy servant be" (2 Sam. 15: 21). And He will surely answer, as that same David did to another fugitive who came to identify himself with his cause: "Abide thou with me, fear not; for he that seeketh my life seeketh thy life, but with me thou shalt be in safeguard." We partake of his sufferings, and He of ours. If anything is too small to tell Him about, it is too small to worry over; but if things worry and fret you, remember that in all your affliction He was afflicted, and that when the Sauls persecute the Church they in reality touch the apple of his eye.

Is it not fit that we should follow our Captain? Would it be right for Him to sink fainting beneath his cross, whilst we are carried to heaven on beds of down? Shall He go through seas of anguish, and we pass round them by a safer and easier path? Shall He be beset by enemies, whom we skilfully elude and avoid, leaving Him to his fate? It must not be. If in the days of his flesh each member of his natural body shared in the suffering of the whole, feet and hands and head contributing their quota, but none exempted, so each member of his mysti-cal body may expect to share still in his sufferings, re-jection, and crucifixion, throughout the course of the ages as they pass.

(6) *Look on to the end.*—His glory shall be revealed! His sufferings quicken our anticipations of that blessed day. Too much comfort might make us forget ourselves and think ourselves at home, so that we might not so ardently reach out our hands towards our coming glories. Hence it is good to have been afflicted, because we have

been taught to consider more fixedly the certainty and glory of the revelation of our hidden Lord. That is the reality; all things else are the baubles and gewgaws of an hour. And when He appears, we shall appear with Him in glory. Those who have been nearest the cross shall be next the throne. The light of his glory shall also irradiate us. We shall be like Him, and with Him, and in Him, for ever. In proportion to our sufferings shall be the rewards and honours of his kingdom. Ah, what bounding and leaping joy will be ours then, in comparison with which the sufferings of the present will seem unfit to be remembered!

(7) *We are compensated for such suffering by the presence of the Spirit of glory.*—When such suffering lies heavily on the soul, God sees to it that it is no loser. What is lost from without is replenished from within. As water is thrown on the fire from the one side of the wall, a bright angel on the other pours in oil through a tiny aperture, till the flame breaks out as coals of juniper. Ah, what compensations are ours! As the spiritual man turns from the hatred of men to the special bestowments of God: he is compensated a hundred-fold. When we have least of human love, we have most of God's. When father and mother forsake, He gathers us. When the sun of earthly prosperity sets, we are sensible of the glowing fire in the heart of the pillar of cloud, which otherwise we had never beheld, and which bespeaks his presence and care. Men can never understand this. They only see the prickly shell, not the kernel. They only handle the rough exterior case; they know not the spices and balm hidden within. They can measure what we renounce, but they cannot gauge the wealth of the Divine compensations. You will never know so much of God's converse as when men "send you to Coventry." You will never have so much of the Spirit of glory and of God as when familiar faces are averted, and hands are raised in scorn. Methinks we are more than repaid for all our losses by this far more exceeding and eternal weight of glory.

Let us brace ourselves then to suffer whatever may befall, only anxious that our sufferings are due, not to our want of Christianity but to our possession of it; not because of temper, or evil-speaking, or misbehaviour, but because we are so like the Master, and so near Him. So like Him that we are mistaken for Him. So near Him that we are bespattered by mud flung at Him.

Not as a murderer, or as a thief, or as an evil doer, but as a Christian. It would be well indeed if we never suffered save as Christians; and whenever such suffering comes to us, let us count it all joy, and take it as the theme for a psalm; as the signal for a fresh outburst of "Glory to God in the Highest!"

26

UNANSWERABLE QUESTIONS

"For the time is come that judgment must begin at the house of God: and if it first begin at us, what shall the end be of them that obey not the gospel of God? And if the righteous scarcely be saved, where shall the ungodly and the sinner appear?"—1 PETER 4: 17, 18.

Stormy times were already breaking on the Church as the Apostle penned these words. Such times had been repeatedly predicted by the Lord, but until now they had not been allowed to break forth in all their terror. A Divine restraint had been laid on the antagonistic influences which lay in wait for the moment in which they should be slipped from their leash. But there was every reason to believe that further respite would be very brief—"The time is come when judgment must begin at the house of God."

Bitter as they are, such times are needed—needed as the north-east wind to break off the dead and useless timber in the spring; needed as the winnower's fan to separate the chaff from the wheat. Without these searching times of judgment, the Church becomes filled with those who make a profession of godliness, but deny its power; whilst without them even the godly and genuine are apt to become too luxurious and self-indulgent, wrapt in slumber, and indifferent to the needs of the world. So from time to time it is needful for God to set Himself to the work of discrimination, of crisis, of judgment.

But the sufferings of this life, at their worst, are only part of a great mystery of pain and judgment which exists,

154

not here only, but hereafter. The believer in Jesus has nothing to fear from that. Whatever may be his present sufferings, they cannot pass the limit of this mortal life; they have no power to send one single stab or thrill over the barrier which separates the two worlds. With the ungodly it is not so. The tempest which breaks on their heads in this life is but the beginning of their sorrows. Through death they pass to greater misery. They depart accursed into fire. They are cast into outer darkness. They are reserved unto a further day of judgment to be punished. Moreover, the sufferings of such as refuse the Gospel are of a very different description, both here and hereafter, to those of God's children. There is the sting of remorse, the reproach of conscience, the bitter sense of severance from God, and love, and hope, and blessedness. Though the believer may suffer, his heart brims with hope; but the heart of the worldling is filled with darkness, the midnight of the soul.

His main end in adverting to the matter at all is with the view of comforting these troubled saints. If, says he, you suffer in time, remember that you will have an eternity of respite. If you suffer as children, rejoice that you will never have to suffer as enemies. If you pass through the deep dark waters of judgment, be sure that your lot is very different from what it would be if you were ungodly and profane. Great though your sufferings may be, they are not to be compared with those of such as reject the Gospel. And, standing on the edge of your own sorrows, you may peer into the seething abyss of theirs, which is indeed a bottomless pit, swathed in mist. And then he concludes this paragraph of suffering with sweet and helpful words about the committal of the soul to God.

I. THE LOT FROM WHICH WE HAVE BEEN SAVED.—There are three gradations or phases of rebellion mentioned here: the disobedient, the ungodly, the sinful. Thus does the spirit pass from the negative condition of carelessness to the positive position of rejection. And in its course it treasures up for itself wrath against the day of wrath, and revelation of the righteous judgment of God. If you obey not the Gospel, you are classed with the ungodly and the profane.

And if such shall read these words, let them consider how certain and awful must be their doom. We are not speaking now of idiots or heathen, or of those who

155

knew not, and yet did commit things worthy of stripes. An infallible authority has told us that they shall be beaten with but few stripes. Our address is to those who have heard the dying words of Jesus, but have turned away from them unmoved, not because they *cannot believe,* but because they *will not,* preferring darkness to light, sin to goodness, self to God.

You have seen the righteous suffer, and how difficult they have found it to endure. Though sustained by the presence of God, and the promises of the Gospel; though assured of the certainty and glory of their reward; though able to read love's message in each stroke, and to see the speedy end of all discipline in heaven's azure calm —yet they have only just been able to keep heart and flesh from despair. But how will it be with you when the hour of your sorrow comes, as it will come, here or hereafter? You will have no presence of God to cheer you, no promises on which to lean, no certainty of a speedy termination, no testimony of a good conscience, no prospect of release. Before you only the certain fearful looking for of judgment and fiery indignation, which shall devour the adversaries. "Can thine heart endure, or can thine hands be strong, in the days that I shall deal with thee?"

If the children suffer so, with all the alleviation of a Father's love, what will not the rebels suffer! If the sufferings of saints be so heavy, what of those of sinners? If the sufferings of this life are often so terrible, what will those of the next be? If the beginning be fraught with so much anguish, how about the end?

It was the earnest wish of a holy man that his death might be so triumphant that his unconverted sons might be convinced and attracted by the evident power of the Gospel to sustain and cheer in the dark passage of the valley. Instead of this, to his deep regret, his spirit lay under a cloud; he was oppressed with fear and misgiving; and the enemy was permitted to torment him to the uttermost. But these very facts were the ones which most profoundly impressed his children. "For," said the eldest, "we all know what a good man our father was; and yet see how deep his spiritual sufferings were. What then may *we* not expect, who have given no thought to the concerns of our souls?"

Besides, consider all that required to be done before the righteous could be saved. Expenditure, such as taxed the resources of Divine Omnipotence. An atonement, which could only be achieved by the death in a human body of the infinite God. The gift of the Holy Spirit Himself, to enter and possess corrupt and wayward hearts, winning them to Himself. All the marvellous interpositions of Providence; the teachings of Scripture; the strivings of conscience. And yet, notwithstanding all, how little is effected in many of God's children! Christian character seems to resemble Chat Moss, which swallowed tons on tons of earth apparently in vain, till the contractors began to despair of ever making even a thin railway embankment across the treacherous bog.

In nature we see glowing worlds, gigantic orbits, vast mountains, noble oceans in their gleaming expanse, cataracts, forests, waterfalls—all worthy of God. But when we come to the moral and spiritual side of his people's character, in spite of all that He has done, we are astonished at the meagre result. They are saved at tremendous cost, and they certainly hardly seem to repay the outlay to which the ever-blessed God has gone.

But if, after all that has been done in them and for them, they are no further forward than they are, what will be the condition of those who remain where the righteous were once, and who have rejected the gracious operations of the Most High? They are charged with sin, with no part or lot in the redemption which the Saviour wrought. They are subject to the abominable pollution of inbred corruption, without the counteracting influence of the Divine Spirit. They are indifferent to those blessed provisions which have engaged the attention of the ever-blessed Trinity from all eternity and rush heedless into the other world. "Where will they appear?"

There are several of these dread unanswered questions in the Bible. "What will ye do in the day of visitation, and in the desolation which shall come from far?" Again: "Who can stand before his indignation, and who can abide in the fierceness of his anger?" And again: "How shall we escape, if we neglect so great salvation?" But amongst them all there is not one more terrible and unanswerable than this: "Where shall the ungodly and sinner appear?"

We can only answer the question in the negative. They will not appear in the clouds when Jesus comes again: only his saints will come with Him. They will not appear at the marriage supper of the Lamb: only the blood-washed can enter there. They will not appear on the right hand of the Judge: only the righteous are found

there. They will not appear among the blessed throngs
of the golden city: for thither entereth nothing that de-
fileth. But when we have ransacked all these places in
vain, we have not answered the inquiry as to their abiding
place. We must leave this for the solemn light of eternity
to disclose.

Oh for tears of blood to weep over their fate! But let
us mingle notes of thanksgiving, that we shall never,
never know it. We cannot perish. We are the objects,
as they might be, of an unchangeable love which cannot
be thwarted. Bought by the blood, taught by the Spirit,
the subjects of the mighty power of God, we shall yet
be more than conquerors. Troubled, but not distressed ;
perplexed, but not in despair ; cast down, but not de-
stroyed ; staggering, but not falling to our eternal destruction ; on the edge of destruction, but brought safe
home on the shoulders of the Good Shepherd. Well
might Dr. Cæsar Malan say to Dr. Gray, turning suddenly
on him, when walking with him at Geneva: "Brother,
you would not go to heaven if you could help it" ; and
then, in answer to a look of surprise, added: "But,
brother, you must go, for Jesus will not let you go elsewhere."

II. THE METHOD SUFFERING SAINTS SHOULD ADOPT.—First,
Be sure that you keep in the current of the will of God.
—"Suffer according to the will of God." Do not go out
of your way to incur trouble. Refuse to fling yourselves
from the mountain brow at the suggestion of the tempter. Dare not to go far afield from under the canopy of
the stately pillar-cloud. Accept all that comes in the natural course of things, but do not sow harvests of pain
by presumption or wrong-headedness, or any form of
evil-doing.

(2) Secondly, *Go on doing well.*—"In well-doing." Do
the next thing. Even if maligned, traduced, or misunderstood, persevere in doing well. It does not matter how
your good deeds are received by men. If you are like
God, you will find them received with contempt and
ingratitude. But your sun must still shine and your
showers fall on the evil and the good, on the just and
on the unjust. You serve the Lord Christ. Live to please
Him.

(3) Thirdly, *Commit the keeping of your souls to God.*
—Our dying Lord committed Himself to Him that judgeth righteously. "Father," he cried, "into thy hands I

commit my spirit." And God has vindicated Him. Let us, in life and death, place our souls, our honour, our good name and standing, our prospects and future, without reserve or question, in the hands of God. He is faithful. Creation is witness to his faithfulness. The stars return with unerring punctuality. Seed-time and harvest, summer and winter, do not cease. He satisfies all instincts which He has implanted. He hearkens to every cry which He has instilled. And, therefore, with unerring love and power He will respond to every appeal made to Him by his suffering ones. He who created is faithful to keep those who commit themselves to Him ; as He who provided the Atonement is faithful and just to forgive those who confess their sins. "He will redeem their soul from deceit and violence ; and precious shall their blood be in his sight."

Safe and strong, tender and true, are the hands of our faithful God. Drop down into them, they will catch you, and sustain your burdens and yourselves. They can hold the oceans in their hollow ; but they are scarred with Calvary's nails. Weary, tired, suffering ones, lie still! none shall pluck you out of the Father's hands. Without anxiety or alarm you may look out from them on the wreck of matter and the crash of worlds. Those hands shall ultimately bear you, as they did your Lord, through all the heavens, and set you down at his own right hand in glory.

27

GOD'S FLOCK AND ITS SHEPHERDS

"The elders therefore among you I exhort, who am a fellow-elder, and a witness of the sufferings of Christ, who am also a partaker of the glory that shall be revealed: Tend the flock of God which is among you, exercising the oversight, not of constraint, but willingly, according unto God ; nor yet for filthy lucre, but of a ready mind ; neither as lording it over the charge allotted to you, but making yourselves ensamples to the flock. And when the Chief Shepherd shall be manifested,

ye shall receive the crown of glory that fadeth not away."
—1 PETER 5:1-4 (R.V.).

A veteran shepherd is speaking here! As he feels his
own strength waning, his heart is away in his loved
work, and he is deeply concerned lest it should suffer.
The ruling passion is strong even unto death!

Imagine a shepherd's hut far away among the northern
hills; stretched on his hard mattress an old shepherd is
dying; the strong frame racked with bronchitis; every
breath laboured and drawn with pain; fever rapidly con-
suming his life. Around him stand his sons, inured to
peril and hardship. The night which hangs over hill and
vale shall not break up under the silver touch of dawn,
ere that strong and noble spirit has passed forth to the
home for which it has long pined. Bend low and catch
his whispered words; mark how they concern the sheep
of his care, as he commends them to his boys: "Lads,"
says he, "mind the flock."

I. WE GET A VIVID GLIMPSE OF THE SIMPLICITY OF THE
CONSTITUTION OF THE EARLY CHURCH.—Wherever God's
people gathered, there was part of his flock. The flock
itself was scattered throughout the whole world, and according to our Master's prayer was *one,* even as it is to-
day. For though there are many folds, there is but one
flock (John 10:16, R.V.). Though some of the sheep are
being led by the living fountains of waters beyond the
river; and others are treading the stony defiles of this
side—yet it is the same flock, bought at the same time,
marked with the same initials, belonging to the same
Owner. And wherever any believers gather, there is a
portion of the one flock, and its officers, teachers, and
spiritual guides are just shepherds, pastors.

How eloquent is this silence as to priestly functions!
Not a word is said as to the necessity of having properly
appointed priests, who should offer a regular sacrifice,
and perform holy rites. In the Apostle's judgment there
was no need to add aught to the precious blood of the
unblemished and spotless Lamb; or to undertake an
office which is being performed through all the ages at the
throne by the great High priest. This would have been
the moment for such a reference, had it been in his mind;
but surely it did not so much as enter his thought. He
was more than satisfied to call himself an "elder," and
to address these simple-hearted men as being on an equal-

ity with himself, with the single exception of their not having, like him, witnessed the sufferings of the Chief Shepherd, by which the flock was purchased (Acts 20:28).

Does not that reference to the sufferings of Christ cast a sidelight on one of the darkest hours of Peter's history? From the fact that he ran in the company of the beloved John to search the empty grave, we may infer that he went to *his* home. when he left the Hall of Judgment with bitter agony of soul. It was too much, however, to stay there alone, while all Jerusalem was astir with the trial and crucifixion of his dearest Friend; and so, when the concourse at Golgotha had emptied the streets, he seems to have stolen forth, making his way by devious by-lanes, till he came on the scene of blood, and, standing afar, was a witness of the sufferings of Christ.

This is the one qualification for tending the flock of God: not to have received a learned education; not to be able to talk glibly or eloquently of spiritual things; not to have been in the imaginary line of apostolic succession—a man may lay claim to all these things, and yet not be competent to feed the flock of God. We must behold, each for himself, the sufferings of Christ; not necessarily with the eye of the flesh, but with the eye of the soul; not with the curious glance of the fickle crowd, but with the fixed loving gaze, which finds in them cleansing for sins and balm for wounds.

And to see those sufferings is not only a qualification for shepherdship, but for glory. As surely as a man beholds those sufferings sympathetically and believingly, so surely shall he behold the glory yet to be revealed. The one is the prelude to the other. No cross, no crown. But where there is the true cross, crown there must be. It may seem to tarry long. The heart may turn sick at the long delay. But that glory which shines now and again as we climb the Transfiguration Mount shall ere long make a perpetual heaven for us when it is revealed.

II. THE CONDITIONS OF SHEPHERDLY CARE.—*Feed* is better rendered *tend,* which includes in one word all the various offices of a shepherd, the leading, feeding, watching, defending. It is not enough to preach to the flock once or twice each week. There must be personal supervision; watching for souls as by those who must give account; seeking them if they go astray; tracking them to the precipice down which they have fallen; and never

161

resting till the straying sheep is brought again to the fold. All this is included in the word; and we need to do all this if we are to tend the flock of God.

The work must be done from love.—If it is undertaken as the result of strong pressure brought to bear on him, or for any reward which may be offered, the shepherd does not fulfil the ideal of this passage. "Not by constraint, but willingly; not for filthy lucre, but of a ready mind." None of God's soldiers are mercenaries or pressed men: they are all volunteers. We must have a shepherd's heart, if we would do a shepherd's work. Nor is this love merely the liking which may come from the flesh, or be dictated by the inclination of the soul. There must be the love which is akin to the love of the Chief Shepherd Himself. A love which can endure without return or thanks; which can grow where there is scarcely any soil; and which clings to the least lovely and thankful. That love is only shed abroad in our hearts by the Holy Spirit. To take the cure of souls only because there is a good living in the family, or for a livelihood, or because it gives position and influence, is a sacrilege which will entail a terrible reckoning for the hireling shepherd.

There is a remarkable addition in the Revised Version —*according unto God;* which serves to accentuate positively what has already been insisted on negatively. God must call to the work; sustain us in it; and give us all the guidance and grace needed for its efficient performance.

It is hard to give up the familiar reading about *God's heritage* in favour of the new rendering, *your allotted portion.* And yet the two expressions are nearly equivalent. For God could not allot that which was not his own. "We are *his* people, and the sheep of *his* pasture." *My flock* is the appellation by which He constantly addresses us. And it is He who allots souls to certain shepherds. Let not those who have small and uninviting charges think lightly of them, since God has entrusted them to their care, and is carefully marking the faithfulness with which the work is done, prepared to reward the true shepherd with a larger charge.

The sphere and people of our ministry should be taken straight from the hands of the Chief Shepherd. We are only accountable to Him. Our work must be done to please Him, and at his direction. We must consult Him about all our plans. We must take His direction as to what part of the green pastures our portion of the flock is to be led into, and by what waters it shall rest. If anything goes wrong we must consider that it should be instantly reported to Him, as the fret and care and burden of direction must certainly be his. If we make mistakes, and the flock suffer through our ignorance, the brunt of the loss must fall on Him. There is no one so interested in the pastor's charge as the Chief Pastor is. He shares all the anxieties, hardships, watchings, and perils of the work. Not to please the flock, not to attract the applause of men, not to gain name and fame, but to do the will of the Chief Shepherd, must be the aim of each true servant of Christ.

And there is to be no *imperious overlording*. We must not abuse our position. The shepherd must win reverence, not compel it. No servant of God must strive, but be gentle unto all, in meekness instructing those that oppose themselves. And since the shepherd, in Eastern mode, must always go before the flock, he must be its *example*. "Be thou an example of the believers," said Paul to the young Timothy, "in word, in conversation, in love, in spirit, in faith, in purity." Those who assume to lead others must be very careful of their behaviour, that they may not be a stumbling-block to any, but that others may be heartened and stimulated by the beauty and consistency of their walk.

Surely, in this conception of the Chief Shepherd there is comfort for those who constitute the flock. When the under-shepherd fails, the Chief Shepherd may be expected to step in to supply his vacated place, or to do his neglected work. Do not grumble to man, but take your complaints to headquarters. And if He does not replace the worthless under-shepherd by another, He will undertake the office of caring for you with his own hands ; and you shall cry, "The Lord is my shepherd, I shall not want." He will see the work done, or do it Himself.

If these words should meet the eyes of any who are away from the tendance of under-shepherds, let me congratulate them on being superintended by the Chief Shepherd Himself. What could be better? The true description of his care is given in his own words, which deserve careful heed. Ezekiel 34:12-16 might almost excite to envy.

III. THE REWARD OF THE FAITHFUL SHEPHERD.—Not the crown of Nemean parsley, destined soon to wither— but of unfading amaranth. A reward for faithful service, which will never grow old, never shrivel, never decay. And thus the memory of the Master's appreciation of the poor service we have rendered will be perpetual. Nor is this all; but some additional strands of glory shall be entwined with the *immortelles*—"the crown of glory that fadeth not away."

Oh liberal recompense! oh, marvellous condescension! oh, rapture of delight! The work itself were reward enough, to say nothing of such a compensation as this. Yet let us strive to win each of the three crowns held out to us. The crown of life to those who endure temptation! The crown of righteousness to those who love his appearing! The crown of glory to those who tend his flock! And in the meanwhile let us ask that He should quickly appear, casting aside the veil which hides Him, and manifesting Himself to eyes that long, and hearts that wait for, his appearing. "Even so, come, Lord Jesus!"

28

THE GARB OF THE HOLY SOUL

"Likewise, ye younger, submit yourselves unto the elder. Yea, all of you be subject one to another, and be clothed with humility; for God resisteth the proud, and giveth grace to the humble. Humble yourselves therefore under the mighty hand of God, that He may exalt you in due time."— 1 PETER 5:5, 6.

One of the chief signs of the unrenewed spirit is the haughty self-complacency with which it bears itself. To resent an insult; to stand upon fancied rights; to vaunt superiority; to show "the silver, and gold, and spices, and precious ointment," in the ostentatious and vainglorious way which brought reproof and chastisement on Hezekiah—this is the manner of the world.

And this insidious sin of *pride* dies hard in the child of God; nay, it may be questioned if ever we shall be perfectly quit of it on this side the gates of pearl. It is Protean in its form, changing with every temperament, suiting itself to every mood, clinging as a Nessus cloak even around the flesh of the converted man. Christian men are proud of their houses, and carriages, and wealth, and position. Christian women are proud of their person,

164

and dresss, and rank, and children. Christian ministers are proud of their influence, and sermons, and the admiration they receive. A bit of flattery, a newspaper notice, a conscious success, are food enough for pride to grow fat upon, till it begins to fancy that all the world is thinking of it, and feels that the most extravagant praise is but a grudging tribute to its worth.

May I not press this upon my readers further, urging each to consider his own character and behaviour in the light of these words. We must be convicted of pride before we seek the grace of true humility. Pride is one of the most detestable of sins; yet does it find lodgment in earnest souls, though we often speak of it by some lighter name. We call it—independence, self-reliance. We do not always discern it in the hurt feeling, which retires into itself, and nurses its sorrows in a sulk. We do not realise how much it has to do with our withdrawing from positions where we feel ourselves outshone by someone who excels us, and with whom we do not care to enter into comparison with the certainty of being second best. It would not be at all easy for us to be silent; to take the lowest place; to learn—where now we count it our prerogative to teach.

And sometimes, when we are clearly worsted, and obliged to step down, we begin to pride ourselves on the sweetness of our disposition in taking the affront so pleasantly. We are proud of our humility, vain of our meekness; and, putting on the saintliest look, we wonder whether all around are not admiring us for our lowliness. I fear me that Bunyan's shepherd-boy, sitting in the lowland glade, and singing, would have become proud of being so low, had he known that his lowliness was to render him immortal. There is at least one preacher whom I know, who has been proud of his sermons on humility, and ostentatious of his efforts to be meek. And thus, even if the soul should array itself in the garb of humility, however simple and plain it be, there is imminent risk of its becoming vain.

"Of all the evils of our corrupt nature, there is none more connatural and universal than pride, the grand wickedness, self-exalting in our own and other's opinion. St. Augustine says truly, *that which first overcame man is the last thing he overcomes*. Some sins, comparatively, may die before us; but this hath life in it, sensibly, as long as we. It is as the heart of all, the first living, the last dying; and it hath this advantage, that whereas other

165

sins are fomented by one another, this feeds even on virtues and graces as a moth that breeds in them, and consumes them, even in the finest of them, if it be not carefully looked to. As one head of this hydra is cut off, another rises up. It will secretly cleave to the best actions, and prey upon them. And therefore there is so much need that we continually watch, and fight, and pray against it, and be restless in the pursuit of real and deep humiliation, daily seeking to advance further in it."

The metaphor used in this passage is surely derived from that most touching incident on the eve of the crucifixion, when, though having present to his mind his origin and destiny, our Lord took upon Him the form of a servant. "Jesus, knowing that the Father had given all things into his hands, and that He was come from God, and went to God; He riseth from supper, and laid aside his garments, and took a towel and girded Himself. After that He poureth water into a basin, and began to wash the disciples' feet, and to wipe them with the towel wherewith He was girded." What a lovely vesture did that stripping, that towel, that lowly attitude, between them make! Not even when He stood radiant on the Mount of Transfiguration did He seem to be dressed so fair. Surely Solomon in all his glory was not arrayed as He. And so the injunction comes to us all, that we should adopt the same livery, and each one don his garb. "Yea, all of you be subject one to another, and be clothed with humility." The question is—how to be humble.

RECOGNISE THE CLAIMS OF THOSE OLDER THAN AND SUPERIOR TO YOURSELF.—"Likewise, ye younger, submit yourselves unto the elder." In Athens it was held to be a matter of first importance that the young should pay deferential respect to their seniors. And even among the precepts of the New Testament, it would be hard to find one more salutary and beautiful than that of the old law: "Thou shalt rise up before the hoary head, and honour the face of the old man, and fear thy God: I am the LORD" (Lev. 19:32).

We need to repeat these maxims of wisdom and grace in the ears of each new generation. It is possible not to notice the great laxity in such matters which is spreading through modern society, loosening its bands, and affecting its stability. Perhaps it is that children are too early taught habits of self-reliance, or are too precocious in their studies. But certain it is that they are more apt

166

to dictate than to submit. Young shoulders are disinclined for the yoke. And yet how many bitter memories are being stored up for coming days! We remember how Dr. Johnson, in late life, stood bareheaded in the rain, in the market-place at Lichfield, in remorseful remembrance of boyish disobedience to his dead father. "Ye younger, submit."

Of course there are occasions when conscience forbids us to submit; and then we must respectfully state the reasons of our refusal, at whatever cost. But these occasions are comparatively rare. And in all doubtful cases —in all cases where a good conscience is not directly infringed—we should submit. Where young Christians have asked my advice as to the way they should behave, when their parents urge them to go to places which, if left to themselves, they would not choose, I invariably answer that, if their conscience absolutely prohibits them, as to the theatre, music-hall, or ball, they have no alternative but to refuse; but, where the question is as to indifferent things. so long as they are under parental control they should yield, if it be insisted on, after they have stated their scruples or objections.

There are, however, other relationships in life besides that of parent and child. We are constantly thrown with those who have seen more of life; have lived more years; and acquired more experience than ourselves: and who have claims upon us. To all such—unless where their character has absolutely forfeited all their claims on our respect—there should be service without servility; meekness without meanness; consideration without cringing; politeness without a thought of policy.

And the cultivation of this habit of deference to those who are older and better than ourselves, with a distinct intention to acquire thereby some new tinge of humility, is to take a considerable step in that direction.

II. TAKE ALL THE OCCASIONS WHICH LIFE AFFORDS OF SERVING OTHERS.—"All of you be subject one to another." Of course there must always be a diversity of function in society; but the very positions in it which we have inherited or acquired give us opportunities of exercising this constant life of self-denial for those around us.

To submit to discomfort, that we may promote their comfort. To submit to inconvenience, that we may make life easier for them. To submit to the cross, that we may save them, though at the cost of our blood. It is the same teaching as came out before in the injunction to "submit to every ordinance of man for the Lord's sake."

Yield before wrong. Hold your mouth in subjection, choking back the proud, resentful words leaping up there for expression and chafing for utterance. Give up even your rights, rather than go to law to keep them. "If any man will sue thee at the law, and take away thy coat, let him have thy cloak also." And submit in such matters, not from mean-spiritedness or cowardice, but because you will accept each opportunity which is put into your way of acquiring the grace of humility.

Let the servant take the rebuke of the master meekly, not careful to vindicate himself, save where the cause of God may be jeopardised by his fault. Let the employé receive the remonstrance of his employer quietly, eager to comply with any righteous demand, and to learn in silence. Let the believer who has said or done anything unkind and unjust to a fellow-believer confess it with shame, and put the scourge into his brother's hands, while he stands meekly to bear the inflicted strokes. Let us not shrink from humbling ourselves before our servants and children, if we have sinned against them. Strong as rocks and lions in our advocacy of the truth as it is in Jesus, let us be as the reed swept by the storm when it is merely a question of our good name, and prestige, and well-being. And let our single purpose be in all to learn the grace of humility, in all the occasions for its practice which our God throws in our way.

III. ACCEPT ALL THE DIVINE DISCIPLINE OF LIFE.— "Humble yourselves under the mighty hand of God." Ah, what infinite sorrow men lay up for themselves in resisting the Divine will! If you fret and chafe against his appointments, finding fault with Him because He has not given you another lot, some other partner for your life, some more congenial occupation, you cannot but be wretched. For at the bottom of all such dispositions, which fume as the waves of the sea, there lurks a feeling of disappointed pride, which thinks that it deserved some better treatment from God, and considers itself ill-used.

But who are we that we demand so fair and comfortable a lot—we whose first father was a gardener who stole his Master's fruit; who have sprung from the dust but yesterday; and who have piled Alps on Andes of repeated sin? Let us accept what God sends. The worst is ten thousand times better than we deserve. The hardest is the better evidence of a love which dares not spoil us. The whole is dictated and arranged by such wisdom as cannot err for a single instant err.

The shadow cast by that mighty hand is dense and dark; its pressure is almost overwhelming. David cried, as he felt it, "Day and night thy hand was heavy upon me; my moisture was turned into the drought of summer." But bend beneath it. Its pressure may be felt in personal suffering, in rebuke, or shame, or persecution, or in loss of property, or in some other form of chastisement, yet take each as another opportunity of putting into practice this injunction to humility.

"Lie still my soul! whatever God ordains is right and good; thou deservest nothing better; what right hast thou to be sitting at the royal table at all, when thou hadst forfeited it for the swine's fare? If thou hadst thy rights, thou wouldst be now in the outer gloom."

IV. OTHER METHODS MAY BE SUGGESTED.—Let us try to get a true estimate of ourselves. Let us judge ourselves now that we be not judged at the last: —

(1) *Look into thyself in earnest*.—"And truly, whosoever thou be that hast the highest conceit of thyself, and the highest causes of it, a real sight of thyself will lay thy crest. Men look on any good, or fancy of it, in themselves, with both eyes, and skip over as unpleasant their real defects and deformities. Every man is his own flatterer. But let any man see his ignorance, and lay what he knows not over against what he knows; the disorders in his heart over against the right motion of them; his secret follies against his outwardly blameless carriage—and it shall be impossible for him not to abase and abhor himself."

(2) *Accustom yourself to look at the good in others*.—Many of us compare ourselves at the best with others at their worst, and of course we come off with advantage, at least in our own esteem. We are so much keener to see the defects than the excellences of our companions. We look at the one with the magnifying glass, and at the other with the reversed telescope. But if we were to be as keen on their virtues as now on their vices, always looking for the compensating grace, always making such allowances as we can find, always magnifying what is lovely and of good report, and thinking of these things,

then we should find the bubbles of our self-congratulation pricked and burst.

(3) *Accept all kind good things from whatever source as the gift of God, and tune your heart in praise to Him.* —It is very pleasant to be thanked and kindly spoken of; to be surrounded by dear friends with their honeyed words: and we may be thankful when such hours shine on us; as it is impossible for them to last, if only we are true to our Master. And whilst they tarry they will not hurt us, if only we pass on all kind speeches in thanksgiving and praise to God. When we can transmute all praises into Praise, all speeches into Speech, and gifts into Sacrifices, falling down to worship Him who is the giver of every good and perfect gift, we shall emerge from the ordeal, without having contracted guilt.

(4) *Claim the humility of Jesus.*—As you go through the world, not only set yourself to resist pride, but make every temptation towards it an occasion for lifting your heart to Christ to receive from Him something more of his own sweet and humble spirit. "Thy humility, Lord!" There are many incitements to this:—

God resisteth the proud.—The Greek word here is very expressive. He set Himself in battle array. Ah, miserable attempt to withstand God. Pharoah perishing in the Red Sea is the perpetual evidence of the futility of the conflict. All things may seem to prosper for a time; but discomfiture is certain, and will be final.

He giveth grace to the humble.—"His sweet dews and showers of grace slide off the mountains of pride, and fall on the low valleys of humble hearts, making them pleasant and fertile. The swelling heart, puffed up with a fancy of fullness, hath no room for grace. The humble heart is most capacious, and, as being emptied and hallowed, can hold most." The vessels which are most heavily laden sink lowest in the water; and those which can sink lowest, without danger, are they which are most heavily freighted. Oh for the humble heart which can hold most grace; and, as it obtains more, sinks still lower in its own esteem!

He will exalt in due time.—"The lame take the prey." The meek inherit the earth. The master of the feast bids those who take the lowest rooms to go up higher. Moses, the meekest man, has taught the principles of jurisprudence to half the world, and sits on the judgment-seat. The martyr's stake has ever been a throne from which the sufferer has ruled after-ages. The men and women

170

of gracious, retiring spirit wield the truest authority in town or village. Those who can die on the cross, pass through the grave to the Ascension Mount. Be humble, not only in outward mien, but in the inner shrine of thy spirit; and in due time, not to-day or tomorrow, but in his own time the Lord will exalt thee to inherit the earth.

29

CARE, AND WHAT TO DO WITH IT

"Casting all your care upon Him; for He careth for you."—1 PETER 5:7.

Every word of this precious verse is golden. And the fact of its standing here as a Divine command is a proof, not only of what is possible for us to do, but of what God is prepared to enable us to do. His commands are enablings; his words are power-words; his light is life. If only you are willing to live this glad, free, uncareful life, and dare to step out on the waves of his carefulness, you will find that, with the resolve to obey, there will come from Him the wondrous power that makes obedience possible.

And it is in the highest degree necessary to obey this precept. So only can we be peaceful and strong. We cannot stand the strain of both work and worry. Two things come between our souls and unshadowed fellowship with God, *sin* and *care*. And we must be as resolute to cast our care on the Lord as to confess our sins to Him, if we would walk in the light as He is in the light. One yelping dog may break our slumber on the stillest night. One grain of dust in the eye will render it incapable of enjoying the fairest prospect. One care may break our peace and hide the face of God, and bring a funeral pall over our souls. We must cast *all* our care on Him, if we would know the blessedness of unshadowed fellowship.

But, besides the blessedness we lose in giving way to care, we must remember that such behaviour sorely grieves and dishonours God. It grieves Him, as love must grieve when suspected of insincerity. And it also sorely dishonours Him. We judge a parent by the report given of him in the words and behaviour of his children.

171

If they seem half-starved and miserable, or look wistfully to us for a dole of help, or complain bitterly of the hardships of their lot, we conclude—however wealthy he may be as to his income, or munificent as to his gifts —that he is hard and cruel: and we withdraw from him as far as possible. So, if the world judges of God by the looks and words of many of his professed children, is it wonderful that it is less attracted than repelled? Either there is no God, or He is powerless to help, or He does not really love, or He is careless of the needs of his children—such must be the reflections of many, as they look on the weary, careworn, anxious faces of God's professed people, and remark in them the same long deeply-ploughed furrows as the years have made for themselves.

We are either libels or Bibles; either harbour-lights or warning signals; either attractions or detractors; and which we shall be depends very much on what we do with CARE.

Of course there must ever be the discipline and chastisement of life. Our Father deals with us as with sons: and what son is he whom the Father chasteneth not? And these strokes of his rod, these cups mingled by his hand, must be bitter to the flesh. But all this is very different from "care." There may be pain—but no doubt of the Father's love, no worry about the issues, no foreboding as to the long future, which to the eye of faith shines like the horizon-rim of the sea on which the sun is shining in its utmost splendour, while dark clouds brood overhead.

Care, according to the Greek word, is that which divides and distracts the soul, which diverts us from present duty to weary calculations of how to meet conditions which may never arrive. Fret; worry; anxiety; the habit of anticipating evil; crossing bridges before we reach them; the permission of foreboding fears about the future; all that attitude of mind which broods over the mistakes of the past and dwells on the shadows which coming events may cast, rather than on the love and will of God—*this is Care*.

I OUR TREATMENT OF CARE.—*Casting all your care upon Him*.—The Greek verb indicates not that we must keep doing it, but do it once for all.

Who does not know what it is to awake in the morning with a sense of heaviness and depression, and, before one is well aroused, to be conscious of a voice whispering a long tale of burdens to be carried, and difficulties to be met, as the hours pass on!

"Ah," says the voice, "a miserable day will *this* be."

"How so?" we inquire, fearfully.

"Remember, there is that creditor to meet, that skein to disentangle, that irritation to soothe, those violent tempers to confront. It is no use praying, better linger longer where you are, and drag through the day as you may. You are like a victim in the tumbril going to be guillotined."

And too often we have yielded to the suggestion. If we have prayed, it has been in a kind of hopeless way, asking God to help, but not daring to think He would. There has been no assurance, no confidence, no calm within, no tranquillity without. Alas for some! They always spend their lives thus. One long, weary monotone of anxiety—struggling against winds and waves, instead of walking over the crests of the billows; treading a difficult, stony pass, instead of being borne along in one of the twenty thousand chariots of God.

How infinitely better to cast our care upon the strong, broad shoulders of Christ! Treat cares as you treat sins. Hand them over to Jesus one by one as they occur. Commit them to Him. Roll them upon Him. Make them his. By an act of faith look to Him, saying, "This, Lord, and this, and this, I cannot bear. Thou hast taken my sins; take my cares: I lay them upon Thee, and trust Thee to do for me all, and more than all, I need. I will trust, and not be afraid." As George Herbert says so quaintly in his sonnet, Put care into Christ's bag. There is no surer path to rest than to pass on to Jesus all the anxieties of life, believing that He takes what we give at the moment of our giving it; that it instantly becomes a matter of honour with Him to do his best for us: and surely it is a sacrilege to take back any gift which we have put into his hands. "Blessed be the Lord, who daily beareth our burden" (Psa. 68:19, R.V.).

There are two or three preliminaries before this committal of care is possible. We must have cast our sins before we can cast our cares; in other words, we must be children in the Father's home. Then also we must be living in God's plan, sure that we are where He would have us be, camped under his brooding pillar-cloud. And, in addition, we must have yielded up our lives to Him, for Him to have his way in them. Nor must we neglect to feed our faith with promise. Without her natural food she pines. But when these conditions are fulfilled, it is not difficult to:

> ". . . kneel, and cast our load,
> E'en while we pray, upon our God,
> Then rise with lightened cheer."

The cup may still have to be drunk, the discipline borne, the work done; but the weary ache of care will have yielded to the anodyne of a child's trust in One who cannot fail.

II. DIFFERENT KINDS OF CARE.—*There is care about our growth in grace.*—It is very unreasonable; and yet how common! We fret because we fear that we are not getting on fast enough, and run to and fro in our anxiety to pick up something from other people. As well might a lad in an infant class fret because he may not enter the higher classes of the school. But surely his one business is to acquire the lessons set before him by the teacher. When those are learnt, it will be for the teacher to give him other and harder ones, and to advance him to positions where quicker progress may be made. And it is for us to learn each day the lessons which the Lord Jesus sets us, and to leave to Him the responsibility of leading us forward in the knowledge and love of God. Cast the care of your growth and attainments on the great Leader of souls, and be content to sit at his feet, learning the lessons He assigns.

There is care about our Christian work.—How to maintain our congregations? How to hold our own amid the competition of neighbouring workers? How to maintain the efficiency and vigour of our machinery? How to adjust differences between our fellow or subordinate workers? How to find material enough to supply the incessant demand for sermons and addresses? How to shepherd a large flock of souls? What elements of care are hidden in each of these! And in what numberless cases the look of weary anxiety betrays the heartache within!

But one is inclined to ask sometimes, *Whose work is it?* If it is yours, resting on your shoulders only, there may be some reasonableness in the carrying of care. But if, as is surely the case, the work is your Master's, the burden should be his also. The prime worker is not you, but Christ. He is working through you. You are but his servant. All that you are responsible for is to do what He bids to the uttermost of your power; and He must bear all the cost and responsibility beside. If things are not going smoothly, go and tell Him, and cast all the anxiety of it back on Him, leaving it to Him to extricate or reinforce you.

There is care about the ebb and flow of feeling.—Our feelings are very changeable. They are affected by changes in the weather and temperature, by the state of our digestion and liver, by over-weariness, by want of sleep by a thousand nameless causes. No stringed instrument is more affected by minute changes than we are; and we are apt to worry when the tide of emotion is running fast out, defying our efforts to retain it. But, if we are not conscious of any sin or negligence to which this subsidence of emotion may be attributed, we may cast the care of such an experience on our Saviour. He knows our frame; and, as we pass down the dark staircase, let us hold fast to the hand-rail of his will, willing still to do his will, though in the dark. "I am as much thine, and devoted to Thee, in the depths of my being now, as when my heart was happiest in thy love."

There is care about household and commercial matters.—Servants, with their frequent changes; employers, with unreasonable demands; customers and clerks; creditors and debtors; children, with the ailments of childhood, and the waywardness of youth. To mention any one of these is to touch a bitter spring of care. There are some whose businesses are specially liable to cause anxious worrying thoughts. Many Christians always think that they must come to beggary; they refuse to enjoy the good things within their reach, because of certain dreaded possibilities. But each of these sources of worry may become a means of grace, a bond between Jesus and the soul. if placed at his feet, and definitely entrusted to his care.

Do not be satisfied with rolling yourself on God, roll your burden also. He who can carry the one can carry the other. When a tiny boy, trying to help his father move his books, fell on the staircase beneath the weight of a heavy volume, his father ran to his aid and caught up in his arms boy and burden both, and carried them in his arms to his room. And will God deal worse with us? He cannot fail or forsake. He can smite rocks, and open seas, and unlock the treasuries of the air, and ransack the stores of the earth. Birds will bring meat, and fish coins, if He bid them. He takes up the isles as a very little thing—how easily, then, your heaviest load: while there is nothing so trivial but that you may make it a matter of prayer and faith.

So Leighton says:—"When thou art either to do or suffer anything, when thou art about any purpose of business, go, tell God of it, and acquaint Him with it—yea, burthen Him with it—and thou hast done for matter of caring. No more care, but sweet, quiet diligence in thy duty, and dependence on Him for the carriage of thy matters. Roll over on God, make one bundle of all; roll thy cares, and thyself with them, as one burden, all on thy God" (Psa. 37:5).

III. THE REASONABLENESS OF THIS METHOD OF LIFE.—"For He careth for you." Of course, if we persist in acting only for ourselves, we must do the best we can for ourselves; but if we can hand over all matters to God, we shall find that He will do infinitely better for us than we had dared to hope. Such is God's love to us that He always goes far beyond our farthest anticipations. "Exceeding abundantly above all that we ask or think."

If the father is providing for to-morrow's needs, why should his little boy leave his play, and lean pensively against the wall, wondering what had better be done? If the pilot has come on board, why should the captain also pace the deck with weary foot? If some wise, strong friend, thoroughly competent, has undertaken to adjust some difficult piece of perplexity for me, and if I have perfect confidence in him, and he assures me that he is well able to accomplish it, why should I fret longer? The thing is as good as done, since he has taken it in hand.

Doubtless there seems a marvellous chasm between *Him* and *you*. But it is bridged by the silver arch of Divine care. God cares for you so much that He came Himself in the person of his Son to redeem you; there was never a time He did not love you, brood over you, and care for you. He cares for you so much as to listen to your least sigh or cry amid the beat of heavenly music and the acclamations of the blessed. The mighty heart of Deity itself is full of a fathomless carefulness for all that concerns you. No mother cares over her sick child as He over you. Each movement and need and desire is read long before expressed or even felt.

Let us trust Him. Tongue cannot tell the completeness, the delicacy, the tender thoughtfulness of the care that will gather and shelter us, as the nervous, careful hen gathers her brood under her wing. "I would have you without carefulness."

30

CONFLICT

'Be sober, be vigilant; because your adversary the devil, as a roaring lion, walketh about, seeking whom he may devour: whom resist steadfast in the faith, knowing that the same afflictions are accomplished in your brethren that are in the world.'—1 PETER 5 : 8, 9.

It would appear that the image of the flock is still in the Apostle's thought; and that he recalls some such incident as that narrated by David, when as a stripling he stood before Saul and related how, as he kept his father's sheep, there came a lion and took a lamb out of the flock; and that he went after him, and smote him, and delivered it out of his mouth, and caught him by the beard, and slew him. However safely folded and watched, no flock is secure against the attempt of the beasts of prey which infest the wilderness. Especially at night they will prowl around, seeking for the unguarded spot, or the unwary sheep, and filling the night with their terrible roarings.

The figure of the lion roaring around the flock reminds us of a rendering given by some to one of God's earliest words to men, when He warned Cain that sin, like a wild beast, was crouching at the door of his heart, waiting to spring in. And we may not forget how our Lord described the coming of the wolf to the flock entrusted to the hireling shepherd, filling him with panic, and resulting in the catching and scattering of the sheep. Satan is evidently no myth, no imaginary being, to the writers of the New Testament. From the distinct references made to him by our Lord to the last great conflict described in the Apocalypse, when he is finally vanquished, there is abundant and emphatic evidence that, behind the veil of the visible, he is heading a great revolt against

177

the rule of God, and is pledged to do his worst by stratagem or skill against his dominion and his saints. It is a subtle manœuvre of his to lead men to suppose that there is no devil at all. A gang of thieves is never so dangerous as when they have it widely rumoured that they have left the neighbourhood. Any artifice succeeds which throws us off our guard.

There is no need to suppose that all God's people are watched and attacked by the devil himself ; for this would almost invest him with the attributes of omniscience and omnipresence. But he is supported and abetted by myriads of wicked spirits in the heavenly places, any of which waits to do his will and to execute his plans ; and the entire host, with long experience of the frailties of human nature, with desperate malice against God, with unwearied watchfulness to do us harm, rests not day or night, but goes to make up that one malign and terrible adversary of which the Apostle speaks. And, indeed, we might relinquish all hope of being able to withstand his onsets, did we not know that he has been vanquished by our Leader, who is prepared to overcome him again, in and through and for each of those who put their trust in Him. O Victor of the Garden, the Cross, and the Resurrection morning, as Thou didst overcome Satan in thine earthly sojourn, so overcome him again in each of us that we may be more than conquerors, because He that is in us is greater than he that is in the world!

I. THE DESCRIPTION HERE GIVEN OF THE TEMPTER.—*He is our adversary.*—The prophet Zechariah was not mistaken when he beheld Satan, standing as an adversary beside the high priest clothed in his dishevelled robes, and standing there to resist him. For, when the veil is drawn aside, in the majestic prologue to the Book of Job, Satan is discovered suggesting an evil and mercenary motive for the uprightness of the patriarch. "Doth Job serve God for nought? Put forth thine hand now, and touch all that he hath, and he will curse Thee to thy face." And thus, when he was cast out of the Heavenlies, as a prelude to his being cast down into the bottomless pit, it is not to be wondered at that loud voices were heard rejoicing that the accuser, who accused the saints night and day before God, had been cast out. But the defeats which he has met with already have only exasperated his hatred the more, and he now roams the earth in all the greater wrath, because he knows that a limit has been put upon his power, and that he hath but a short time.

He roars as a lion.—There is terror in his threatenings, which may well strike panic into timid hearts. But we must remember that it is the expending of ineffectual rage. He makes up in noise what he has lost in power. He hates our Shepherd, though he cannot now hurt Him. He did his worst against Him, and failed. He must content himself with bellowing out his hate; though this, too, shall be stayed. So Rutherford used to say that he preferred dealing with a roaring devil. It fills Satan with redoubled chagrin and malignity to know that the weakest saint is more than a match for him, if he dares to resist him, steadfast in the faith, and armed in the panoply of God. "My sheep," said the Chief Shepherd, "shall never perish."

He walketh about seeking.—There is no church-fold which he does not eagerly visit; bent on injuring its usefulness, or snatching away its careless professors. No bishop so busy in his diocese as he. If only he can vitiate Christian teaching by false doctrine, so that every sermon may carry with it error enough to cancel its truth and power; if he can involve the leading professors in inconsistencies which shall neutralise the effect of their testimony; if he can entrap the weaklings into pride, or jealousy, or sensual pleasure, or backsliding; if he can scatter the flock by persecution, or bury it in a snowstorm of formalism, or drown it in a spate of worldliness, then he is full of glee. And he is always on the watch for such a chance. "Going to and fro in the earth, and walking up and down in it."

Satan considers the saints. "Hast thou considered my servant Job?" No neglect of the morning watch, no permission of the first faint thoughts of evil, no unwatchfulness, no tampering with wrong, escapes his attentive scrutiny. He never yet missed an opportunity of following up any clue, or making the most of any advantage. We are engaged in conflict with an accomplished and merciless opponent, who is quick to plunge in his sword wherever the joints of the armour open, and whenever we give him the chance. What need, then, for constant vigilance on our part to meet and parry his attacks! "Be sober! be vigilant!" And what need also for the ceaseless intercession of Him who sees the approach of temptation. and anticipates it by his prayers! "Simon, Simon, behold, Satan hath desired to have you, that he may sift you as wheat: but I have prayed for thee, that thy faith fail not."

II. THE AIM OF SATANIC TEMPTATION.—When the devil tempted our Saviour, He could truthfully say, "The prince of this world cometh, and hath nothing in Me." But only *He* could say this. In all else there is a certain proneness to go wrong, to which the great adversary makes his appeal. And before we can hope to vanquish assaults from without, we must be careful to have taken up that attitude with respect to the inner realm which is ours in the holy arrangements of God. We cannot successfully vanquish assaults from without, whilst there is revolt or anarchy within. And for this reason the Apostle has been careful, at the commencement of the previous chapter, to deal with the question of the flesh. For only when we have truly experienced what God is prepared to do in relation to the flesh, shall we be able to stand in his grace against our terrible adversary, or maintain the attitude of uncompromising vigilance and unremitting watchfulness. Perhaps there is, as Bengel suggests, a hint of this in the admonition, *Be sober!*

When man first came from his Maker's hand, all his natural appetites and desires, which in themselves were pure and necessary, were under the control of the will, which itself was true to God, willing only what God willed, and obeying each prompting of his Spirit. But man swerved from the blessed condition, substituting self for God, and his own pleasure for obedience to the Divine law and will. And ever since that one fatal act there has been transmitted to all after-generations a bias towards evil, a tendency to repeat that first sin in aggravated forms, a predisposition to the gratification of natural instincts, irrespective of the Divine requirements. This inherited tendency is due to the operation of that great principle which scientific men know as the law of heredity, and which operates through all races of the creatures with which we are familiar in our world-home.

The sphere in which this inherited tendency mostly manifests itself is in relation to the appetites and desires of the body, the natural action of which has been much interfered with through successive generations, and which, as they come to us, bear evidence of the abuses to which they have been subjected by our progenitors. Now, of course, these natural impulses, though vitiated in their operation, cannot constitute sin until they have inflamed the imagination, captured the heart, and conquered the will. But, as a matter of fact, there is not one of us in whom they have not done all these things again and again, and in doing so have increased and accentuated our susceptibility to evil. This perverted tendency of our appetites, coupled with its inevitable influence on the inner life, is what the Word of God calls *the flesh*. "The flesh, with the passions and lusts" (Gal. 5:24). "We all had our conversation in times past, fulfilling the desires of the flesh and of the mind" (Eph. 2:3).

God has judged this flesh in the person of Jesus, made in the likeness of sinful flesh, and has assigned it to the cross. There, on Calvary, is God's verdict and doom for the flesh. And in his thought and purpose our flesh has been crucified there. "Our old man was crucified with Him, that the body of sin might be done away" (Rom. 6:6, R.V). Also, "They that are of Christ Jesus have crucified the flesh" (Gal. 5:24, R.V.)—statements which cannot be appropriated by one or two, but are made generally of all the saints, as they are considered in the person of their Representative and Head. Oh that there were not, through our failure in faith and obedience, so great a gap between what all the saints are in the purpose and thought of God, and what they are in their practical realisation!

But God has done more than assign "flesh" to the cross. He has given us his Holy Spirit, whose special office it is to restore to the inner life, and to the body also, a right-ordered and natural existence. There are some who seem to suppose that He takes the evil bias entirely away, so that they are as Adam before he fell. In our judgment this is contrary to the teaching of Scripture, which recognises the presence of the flesh in believers, though it expressly teaches that they are "not in the flesh." But the Holy Spirit is eager to dwell in each believer mightily, as a counteractive agency, lusting against the flesh, restraining its every manifestation, keeping it utterly in the place of death ; and this so calmly and quietly, that the happy subject of his grace may begin to suppose that the flesh is extirpated or eradicated, when in point of fact it is present still, and would reveal itself, if the gracious operation of the Holy Spirit were restricted for a single moment (Gal. 5:17, R.V.).

It is not a question of what Christ can do, but of what He has undertaken to do. Of course, a moment is coming when we shall put off this body, and when the redemption of our entire being will be completed in the acquisition of a body fashioned in the likeness of our Lord's. But till then we are doomed to carry about a body which is apt, through inclinations excited in the mind, to hurry us into sin (1 Cor. 9:27). Yet surely it is more blessed to have the constant indwelling, restraining, sanctifying grace of the Holy Spirit, as the source of our deliverance from the flesh, than to have back again the nature of unfallen Adam, which might at least fall again before the onset of the tempter.

We once lived in a house, the cellar kitchen of which was so damp that the servant was able sometimes to sweep up the white mould from the tiles; but as long as we kept up a roaring fire, the damp was undiscernable, and the kitchen was warm and pleaant. Indeed, no stranger would have realised how strong the tendency to damp was. But if there was no fire for weeks, or even for days, the damp revealed itself. So, when the Spirit works mightily in the soul, He is like the ruddy glow of a furnace, and the evil tendencies of our nature are as if they were not.

We were informed that the workmen employed in making the subterranean tunnel through London came on a bed of sand, through which water was flowing freely, but they were kept perfectly dry so long as the parts excavated were filled by a strong blast of compressed air. So is the heart kept pure and sweet as long as the Spirit dwells in it in power. It is of the utmost importance, then, to live in the Spirit and walk in the Spirit, that we may not fulfil the lusts of the flesh.

Temptation does not only come from without, as some say. The spark may be flung in from without; but there is a magazine of gunpowder within. The match would be struck on the lid in vain if there were not a prepared surface on which it would ignite. "Every man is tempted, when he is drawn away of his own lust and enticed" (James 1:14). And it is because of the known presence of these evil tendencies within that the devil watches us so closely.

As long as we are kept by the mighty power of God, we are safe. The conflict is no longer within, but without. And all hell shall expend itself in vain on the nature which is experiencing the blessed reign of the Spirit of God, which makes us free from the law of sin and death. Yield yourselves to God; receive the filling of the Holy

182

Spirit by faith; and then march to assured victory through the power of the Son of God.

III. CONSOLATION TO THE TEMPTED.—(1) *Your temptations are not an uncommon experience.*—We have all the same constitution; and there is much more similarity in our temptations than we suppose. "There hath no temptation taken you but such as is common to man." "The same afflictions are accomplished in your brethren that are in the world."

(2) *All temptation is under the restraint of God.*—As in the case of Job, Satan cannot tempt us without God being first acquainted with his designs. And, as in the case of Peter, there seems to be almost a seeking and receiving of permission to tempt before Satan assails. In any case, no temptation befalls us greater than our power to combat and overcome. And we are permitted to be tempted, that we may learn to avail ourselves of the resources of which we might otherwise be unaware.

(3) *Satan can be conquered.*—Watch and pray. Be sober in your tastes and habits, in your words and deeds. Never neglect to abide in your strong fortress, Christ. Keep with the flock of God. Nourish your souls with the Word, that you may be healthy and strong. Gird on the whole armour of God. Resist the first insignificant advances of the foe. Be steadfast in the faith. Look instantly to Jesus to cast the panoply of his protection around you; and to stand between you and your assailant, as a shield before the body of the warrior. Resist the devil, and he will flee from you. Go into battle assured of success: this your talisman, *They overcame by the blood of the Lamb;* this your battle-cry, *Jesus saves, Jesus saves.*

31

THE CALL TO ETERNAL GLORY

"The God of all grace, who hath called us unto his eternal glory by Christ Jesus, after that ye have suffered

awhile, make you perfect, stablish, strengthen, settle you."—1 PETER 5:10.

What a contrast is presented between the attacks referred to in the previous verses, and the all-sufficient grace, which lies as a great depth beneath this!

Why should we fear the attacks of the great adversary of souls, so long as the God of all grace is ours? There is no kind of grace we can need, which does not reside in Him; yea, grace on grace, so that when one supply is exhausted there is always more to follow. And the attacks of Satan are, perhaps, permitted that we may be constrained to realise and avail ourselves of the stores of grace which are treasured up in Jesus Christ our Lord. "In Him dwelleth all the fullness of the Godhead bodily; and in Him ye are made full" (Col. 2:9, 10, R.V.).

Edinburgh Castle, perched on its grey crags, is said to have been captured only once; and then through a shepherd leading a small storming party up the precipitous western cliffs, which had been left undefended because deemed to be inaccessible. And yet there was benefit even in that apparent disaster, because it indicated a weak spot in the defences for all after-time, and led to a more perfect line of fortification. So we may be thankful when temptation assails us, indicating some point of our character which needs immediate attention, and summoning us to look into the Divine storehouse for some special and unrealised form of grace, which from that moment is claimed and appropriated by the exercise of faith.

It is an exceedingly beautiful title: "The God of *all* grace!" Illuminating grace for the seeker; justifying grace for the believer; comforting grace for the bereaved and sorrowful; strengthening grace for the weak and downtrodden; sanctifying grace for the unholy; living grace, and dying grace. Bring hither the pitchers of your need. The grace of God, which is his unmerited love, will conform itself to their special shape, and will seem to be just fitted to your exigencies and requirements. The ocean is known by several names, according to the shores it washes, and its very tints vary with the shades of the rocks that line the margin of its bed; but it is the same ocean, and its waters are identical in every place. So is it ever the same love of God, though each needy one discovers and admires its special adaptation to his need. "The God of all grace."

I. OUR DESTINY.—It is almost too marvellous to credit, and yet it must be so, that He has called us *unto his eternal glory*. He is the giver of all grace; and He calls us to all his glory. We therefore stand in his grace, and rejoice in hope of the glory of God (Rom. 5:2).

We shall ere long behold that glory which is just the shining forth, in all their loveliness, of the manifested attributes of the ever-blessed God. This was our Saviour's request, which carried with it the certainty of realisation. "Father," He said, "I will that they whom Thou has given Me, be with Me where I am, that they may behold my glory." Not on his back parts only shall we look, as Moses did, as the procession swept down the mountain pass; nor for so transient a moment as the disciples beheld his glory when they were with Him on the Holy Mount; but face to face, in prolonged and steadfast fellowship. The Queen of Sheba, contrasting her brief visit to Solomon's court with the lot of his servants who lived there, broke into exclamations of envy at their lot. "Happy are thy men, happy are these thy servants which stand continually before thee." Conceive, then, what our lot is to be through endless ages!

Nor shall we behold it: we shall share it.—"The glory which Thou gavest Me I have given them." Co-heirs with Jesus in all that He has won through his humiliation and death. Sharers in his unsearchable riches; participators in his unspeakable and triumphant joy; one with him in a unity, which in its mystic circle weaves the Deity itself into oneness with redeemed men. "That they may be one, even as we are one: I in them, and Thou in Me; that they may be made perfect in one."

And this glory is *eternal,* not as to the length, but as to the quality of it. For it is difficult to speak of the successions of time, when considering that state of being from which time is expressly eliminated. The word certainly means more than never-ending being. It involves conceptions of the imperishable, the untainted, the altogether satisfying, the Divine. Bread, of which if a man eats, the vast appetite of his spirit is sufficed. Joy, of which he can never tire. Knowledge, which is beclouded by no limiting mystery. Life, which reaches to all the lengths and breadths and heights of that spirit which God has made in the image of his own. Glory, which will meet and far surpass the loftiest desires and anticipations which have ever extorted from any of the elect

185

spirits of our race the cry, "I beseech Thee, show me thy glory."

Tell us not, then, of jasper walls, or golden streets, or flashing jewels. These will no more suffice us than jewels will compensate the bride for the absence of her lord. We are set on attaining the glory to which God has called us in Jesus. And by his dear grace we shall attain it, too ; for we have already received his grace, which is glory in the bud. Nor would our God mock us with the foretaste and earnest unless he were prepared to consummate all his grace with all his glory.

Oh, who will heed this call, which is yet sounding through the world, but which may soon cease? Surely the sons of men cannot realise what obedience to it involves. They think more of what they must give up than of what they are to receive. But if they would reverse this process, and think more of what they are certain to receive in Jesus Christ, methinks they would leave all else, without one anxious thought, in order to follow whither such delights entice.

II. OUR PATHWAY THITHER.— "After that ye have suffered a little while." *Suffering is inevitable*. Through much tribulation we must pass to our reward on high. No cross, no crown ; no Gethsemane, no emptied grave ; no cup of sorrow, no chalice of joy ; no cry of forsakenness, no portion with the great, or spoil with the strong. All who suffer are not necessarily glorified ; but none are glorified who have not somehow suffered. We must drink of his cup, and be baptised with his baptism, if we would sit right and left of the King. The comet that stands longest nearest to the sun must have plunged furthest into the abyss.

Let sufferers take heart! If only their sufferings are not self-inflicted ; if they do not result from their own mistakes and sins ; if they arise from that necessary antagonism to sin and the present world into which close following of the Crucified must necessarily bring any one of us ; if they are borne, not only submissively, but with the heart's choice, as of those that delight to do the will of God—then each pang is a milestone marking their way onwards to the goal of light and glory.

Suffering is necessary to our characters.—The Apostle does not for a moment wish his converts spared from the ordeal. Nothing short of necessity would ever lead God to expose us to the fire. But in no other way can

186

our truest bliss be achieved. In no other school-house are the lessons of obedience so acquired as in that kept by Sorrow. The Lord Himself was once a scholar there, and carved his name on the hard and comfortless boards. In no other ordeal can we lose so much dross; drop so much chaff, learn so much of our own nothingness; be drawn so close to his companionship; or be taught such true estimates of the comparative values of things, weighing the present against the future, till we feel that it is not worthy to be compared with the glory to be revealed.

Suffering is limited.—At the most, it is for but a little while. Remember how often the Lord Jesus repeated the words, it is only "a little while" (John 16:16-19). It was a note on which his fingers lingered, as if loth to leave it. Compared with all the future, the longest life of suffering is only for a moment; and, contrasted with the weight of glory, the heaviest trials are light. Let us not look at the things which are seen, but at those which are not seen. The hills which would daunt the traveller seem diminutive when they are seen lying about the feet of some soaring Alp. Weeping can only stay for the brief summer night, and in the early twilight must hasten veiled away; because joy cometh in the morning, bringing the herald-beam of the long, happy summer day, on which night can never fall or draw her dusky veil.

When once that glory breaks upon us, the separations and misunderstandings and agonies of time will be no more remembered than a pin's prick is recalled by the soldier on the day of his public welcome and decoration.

> *"And when we gain the shore at last,*
> *We shall not count the billows past."*

III. OUR NURTURE IN THE DIVINE LIFE.—All our hope must be in God. We are not to concern ourselves to cope with the difficulties of our growth in grace, or to fret about what seems to be our slow progress. If only we are willing, trustful, and obedient, God will make Himself responsible for all the rest. "God shall *Himself* perfect, stablish, strengthen you" (R.V.).

He shall perfect—i.e., He shall put you in joint, so that his will may work through you, without let or hindrance; as the will of each human being operates consciously through any part of our marvellous nature.

He shall stablish—i.e., He shall found you so massively on the Rock of the person and work of the Lord Jesus, that when the rain descends, and the floods come, and the winds blow, and beat upon you, you may not fall, because rooted and grounded in Him.

He shall strengthen—i.e., He may not take away the suffering or the temptation, but He will give more grace, communicating his own strength; so that the soul may even glorify God for infirmity and trial, and say gladly: "The Lord is my light and my salvation; whom shall I fear? the Lord is the strength of my life; of whom shall I be afraid?"

How safe and strong then may we be, if only we will go again and again to the God of all grace, claiming, with holy boldness, grace to help us in time of need; and believing that it is to us not according to our feeling but our faith! It is not probable that Elisha *felt* any different as he turned back from the chariot of fire, which had swept in between him and Elijah. He looked and felt as in the morning of that day; but a vast change had passed over him, which only awaited the River Jordan to call it forth into marvellous manifestation. So we may not be always conscious of the vast changes which are being gradually effected within us in answer to our faith; but when we approach the bank of some foaming river of difficulty or temptation, our behaviour and victory will open the lips of onlookers to exclaim, "Lo, God is here."

Let us give Him glory! Do not hesitate to tell Him what you think of Him. Amid all the hatred, and blasphemy, and misunderstanding of his foes, let us blend voice and heart in ascribing to Him glory and dominion for ever and ever! Let the notes rise higher and higher as life climbs up towards its goal; until they are merged in the ocean of praise, the billows of which smite against his throne, breaking into the spray of a thousand songs! Thus may it be "for ever and ever." Amen.